HOW TO HELP YOUR SCHOOL THRIVE
WITHOUT BREAKING THE BANK

HOW TO HELP
YOUR SCHOOL
THRIVE
WITHOUT BREAKING THE BANK

John G. Gabriel
Paul C. Farmer

Association for Supervision and Curriculum Development
Alexandria, Virginia USA

Association for Supervision and Curriculum Development
1703 N. Beauregard St. • Alexandria, VA 22311-1714 USA
Phone: 800-933-2723 or 703-578-9600 • Fax: 703-575-5400
Web site: www.ascd.org • E-mail: member@ascd.org
Author guidelines: www.ascd.org/write

Gene R. Carter, *Executive Director;* Nancy Modrak, *Publisher;* Julie Houtz, *Director of Book Editing & Production;* Miriam Goldstein, *Project Manager;* Catherine Guyer, *Senior Graphic Designer;* Mike Kalyan, *Production Manager;* Valerie Younkin, *Desktop Publishing Specialist;* Carmen Yuhas, *Production Specialist*

All Web links in this book are correct as of the publication date below but may have become inactive or otherwise modified since that time. If you notice a deactivated or changed link, please e-mail books@ascd.org with the words "Link Update" in the subject line. In your message, please specify the Web link, the book title, and the page number on which the link appears.

PAPERBACK ISBN: 978-1-4166-0758-8   ASCD product #107042   n2/09

Also available as an e-book through ebrary, netLibrary, and many online booksellers (see Books in Print for the ISBNs).

Quantity discounts for the paperback edition only: 10–49 copies, 10%; 50+ copies, 15%; for 1,000 or more copies, call 800-933-2723, ext. 5634, or 703-575-5634. For desk copies: member@ascd.org.

Library of Congress Cataloging-in-Publication Data
Gabriel, John G., 1973–
   How to help your school thrive without breaking the bank / John G. Gabriel and Paul C. Farmer.
      p. cm.
   Includes bibliographical references and index.
   ISBN 978-1-4166-0758-8 (pbk. : alk. paper) 1. School management and organization. 2. School environment. I. Farmer, Paul C., 1958- II. Title.
   LB2805.G13 2009
   371.2'07–dc22

                                                                            2008042597

8 17 16 15 14 13 12 11 10 09   1 2 3 4 5 6 7 8 9 10 11 12

To my sweet Caroline

My soul, always on my mind

and always in my heart

Your John

To my wife Holly and our three children

Paul, Casey, Katie

They are my life, my blood, my heart, my soul;

I am them, they are me.

Paul

How to Help Your School Thrive Without Breaking the Bank

Acknowledgments

John would like to thank the following people:

There are many people to whom I am grateful, but I first want to express special thanks to my family and friends for their continued support and understanding, both during the writing process and when life just *happens*. It is only because of great family and friends that anything is possible. Above all, I am especially thankful to my lovely wife Caroline for her patience and encouragement.

I am grateful for having been able to work with too many talented teachers to name here, but I would be remiss if I didn't mention a few unique educators whose leadership I value: thank you to Anne Brooks for taking a risk by bringing in a novice administrator; Dr. Virginia Minshew, an inspiring belle of a leader who has taught me to "belle" and with whom I am privileged to be presently taking the journey; Dr. Edgar Hatrick, a leader who motivates me every time I hear him speak; Jeff Adam for his willingness to collaborate and problem-solve; Daryl Cummings for her organizational skills and desire to help students; Beth Walker for her perspective and sharp insight; Bob Marple for being such a good listener who taught me much in a short period of time; Pam Jacobs for her assistance during my first year at PVHS; Mie Devers, whom I wish well as she embarks on her own leadership journey; Erin Mastrangelo, who will make a strong leader if she decides to choose that path; Dr. Vera Blake, who continues to have an impact on me; Paul Farmer, a mentor who hasn't stopped mentoring and who I'm glad decided to give this a chance; the team at ASCD of Scott Willis, Genny Ostertag, Carolyn Pool, and Miriam Goldstein, for their support and feedback; and, of course, Harry, who was always there for me.

Paul would like to thank the following people:
   I would like to express a sincere appreciation to the numerous educators who have touched my life throughout my educational career, starting with my days as a high school student. To Joe Kuhn, my high school automotive teacher and coach, for showing me what it is like to have a teacher who genuinely cares for hard-to-reach students. To Tom Milans, my first department chair, who took the time to help me become a teacher with the skills I dreamed of possessing in the classroom. To Barry Burke, my coordinator in Career and Technology Education, for his meticulous attention to detail and continuous encouragement of my professional growth. To Phil Gainous at Montgomery Blair High School and Vera Blake at Falls Church High School, two outstanding principals who helped me develop the required skills, fundamentals, and characteristics for successful leadership in education. To John Gabriel for giving me an opportunity to join him in his second book and for providing much-needed guidance. And finally, to my wife Holly, my family, and my friends for their continued encouragement and support throughout this process.

Introduction

Helping our schools thrive often means changing the way we do things, which can spark feelings of anxiety. The familiar is always more comfortable. When faced with the prospect of change, those who will be affected tend to scramble to justify their routines, often with the ubiquitous "This is what we have always done." Although such a response is a normal institutional reaction to the threat of change, it's a self-defense mechanism and a rationalization that is rarely in a school's best interest. Rationalizations tend to be rooted in tradition and emotions rather than in measurement and pragmatism. Consciously or otherwise, cultural natives—those who are deeply attached to the current practices, norms, and traditions, even if they are illogical or outmoded—may be preserving the status quo for personal reasons. The present way of doing things—the impact of past leaders and teachers and a school's myths, realities, and artifacts—can be difficult to navigate. If you are reading this book because you want to get the most out of your school, you should know that what you will really be doing is reshaping your school's culture.

Understanding School Culture

Culture can be defined in several ways, but most simply put it is

- What is done;
- Why it is done; and
- How it is done.

Culture is the heartbeat and lifeblood of any school; it is what a school and its inhabitants value, believe, and practice. For better or for worse, newcomers tend to adapt to and perpetuate the culture they find themselves in. Roland Barth (2002) asserts that "probably the most important and most difficult job of an instructional leader is to change the prevailing culture of a school. A school's culture has far more influence on life and learning in the schoolhouse than the president of the country" (p. 6). Therefore, getting the most out of your school is usually not a simple matter of purchasing some new program, but rather of changing the core of the school: moving from how things *are* and *have been* done to how things *should* and *will be* done.

Schools are more than bricks and mortar: they're vibrant, unique learning communities not unlike living, breathing organisms. And as Jan Keating (2006) notes, "If an organism cannot adapt to the changing environment, it will cease to exist. If allowed to change and adapt to fit its environment, the organism will evolve and flourish" (p. 1). For this reason, it is best to avoid categorizing a school's culture as being "positive" or "negative." Rarely will culture remain static or move in only one direction. It's more useful to envision culture as the fluid spectrum depicted in Figure i.1. In the sections that follow, we give brief descriptions of the three types of cultures shown in the figure: benign, ill, and healthy (see Resource 1).

Benign Culture

A benign culture is the most common type of school culture. As the term denotes, such a culture is not detrimental. At the same time, it does not regularly contribute to the optimal well-being of a school; it is stagnant and in need of exercise. Staff members assess one another primarily according to friendliness, and the vast majority of teachers have never observed their peers' professional capacity.

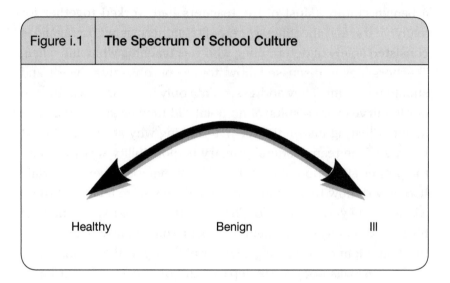

| Figure i.1 | The Spectrum of School Culture |

Healthy   Benign   Ill

Most conversations in a benign culture lack substance, only sometimes drifting to professional content and even then rarely scratching beneath the surface. Those in the school see no reason to change because things are "good enough": students and their work are good enough, teachers are good enough, and administrators are good enough. The leadership in a benign culture is management in disguise because it deals mainly with daily affairs and operations, with no big dreams for the future (or no knowledge of how to execute them). There is no talk of or action taken toward continuous improvement. This attitude may emanate from teachers or administrators, or from both groups in a tacit or spoken understanding. Regardless, students can sense it and are content to merely meet expectations.

Essentially, a school with this kind of culture is in a state of benign neglect. Not enough is being done to challenge established comfort zones and help teachers to grow professionally—to reflect on and refine practices to enhance student achievement.

In a southern Virginia high school of nearly 2,000 students, we knew a social sciences department that had the hallmarks of a benign culture. Most of the teachers had worked together for many years, and meetings were polite gatherings whose agendas consisted solely of determining who was teaching what and when. Teachers never discussed how topics or objectives were and should be taught. They addressed data only in terms of whether or not to curve exam results; at no point did they engage in dialogue about adjusting instruction or determining why students did not fare well. The team leaders' primary responsibility was to ensure the proper allocation of resources. Team members were generally happy with how things functioned, and they were left alone to do whatever they wanted to do. The department chair spent much of his time shielding department members from initiatives and activities that might create pedagogical or philosophical discomfort.

Yet this was not a weak department; on the contrary, it had a respectable passing rate of nearly 88 percent on standardized measurements. The department as a whole just was not interested in improving or in exploring new ways of doing things. The administration never advocated new ideas or initiatives for improvement, instead focusing its efforts on underperforming academic areas. It was content with letting this department coast along rather than helping it excel.

The culture of mediocrity was deemed acceptable, and nearly all stakeholders were complicit in this arrangement. No one expressed a wish to dig deeper into the test scores or to consider that they could improve the way they had been doing things. New teachers with fresh ideas were outnumbered and outvoiced; some even grew to like the anonymity and instructional isolation. Although novice teachers did employ new strategies and ideas that they had learned in their preservice training, they learned not to share them with other department members, who were content enough with what they had always done.

Ill Culture

A small portion of schools inhabit this end of the spectrum. An ill culture is infectious and, if allowed to spread unchecked, may permeate all stakeholders and have a deleterious effect on the organism of the school. Even healthy individuals are susceptible to the metastasizing effect of this virulent force.

Characterized by cynicism, pessimism, and distrust, an ill culture lacks cohesion for the overall good. The school's inhabitants have not reached a common understanding on the purposes of classes, teams, and departments: they are all islands unto themselves. In this thankless culture, the only thing staff members share is a defeatist attitude, and they are quick to point accusatory fingers at others for all that is wrong. These attitudes are often coupled with a lack of accountability that exacerbates the situation.

Leadership in an ill culture is usually held by a few and is not exercised prudently. Decisions tend to be unsupported because school leaders have not taken ownership of them, communicated them sufficiently, or sought staff buy-in. School leaders often use their power and authority to drive their agendas and punish rather than to explore possibilities and build support. Such leadership promotes a climate of fear and strangles the potential of a healthy culture.

We'd like to be wrong, but we're pretty sure that everyone has his or her own horror story of working in an ill culture or at least knows someone who has experienced its spirit-sapping force. We have met talented teachers crushed by the utter lack of collegial and administrative support for disciplinary and instructional issues. In some such cultures, turnover is high, leaving a core of malcontents who poison newcomers with their negative practices and philosophies, thereby perpetuating both the culture and the turnover. Some good teachers believe that things will improve if they can just outlast their poisonous colleagues, but the ill culture takes a toll on their livelihoods and, in some instances, on their personal lives.

We have known teachers in one particular department who actively campaigned against fellow department members not only to other colleagues but also to students and parents. We have been stunned by teachers whose assessments failed to align with the curriculum or objectives and who belatedly entered grades into their grade books, only to forget them. We have encountered administrators who ignored a detrimental situation because they did not believe they could change it. Their lack of effort and accountability had a demoralizing effect on those who did care, who did want things to change, and who struggled to do the right thing.

Any true change to such an environment requires stakeholders to acknowledge the "brutal facts" (Collins, 2001) and make an honest, objective examination of the culture. Unflinchingly acknowledging malignant beliefs, behaviors, and practices is the first step in the rehabilitative process.

Healthy Culture

A healthy culture is marked by integrity and a strong work ethic. In such a culture, people work across departments and professional roles toward common goals and manage to achieve and sustain success. Staff members are collaborative and reflective risk takers who seek to fix things that aren't working and to enhance things that are. By flexing their educational muscles, they challenge themselves, their colleagues, and their students.

In a healthy culture, educators engage in honest, professional dialogue on curriculum, assessments, data, interventions, and remediation. Participants leave meetings having learned something new, or at least feeling reinforced in what they are doing. They are comfortable with their vulnerability in meetings and view suggestions as constructive, not as put-downs or attacks. Without prompting, they turn to one another when facing a problem or seeking a better way to do something. Their practices are transparent and research-based.

However, even a healthy school's inhabitants cannot take its culture for granted. The school needs strong, effective shared leadership teams to maintain its well-being and ensure the development of both students and future leaders. A healthy school is characterized by horizontal leadership: when possible, staff members are given the opportunity to explore and discuss decisions. Without this system of shared leadership, the school runs the risk of atrophy.

In one mid-Atlantic high school we know, the healthy culture stems primarily from the principal. He empowers his assistant principals to make decisions, lead initiatives, and speak and act on his behalf. The administrative leadership team meets quarterly to discuss books and articles that have been assigned to them by the principal. Regular meetings center on data and instructional concerns. The members of the administrative team help one another by brainstorming solutions to problems and collaborating on tasks, and they model these behaviors and expectations to the rest of the staff. Although not everyone likes all of the assistant principals, the staff almost universally respects them.

The school's departments and teams generally follow the administrative team's example of sharing leadership and encouraging professional growth. Some of the weaker teachers are made a little stronger through their colleagues' willingness to observe them and share ideas and strategies. This support structure is a key characteristic of the school's healthy culture. Each department's guiding vision and mission statements were developed through honest, stimulating, and boundary-pushing dialogues.

Getting the Most Out of This Book

Changing a department's or a school's culture is no simple task. In addition, times are always tough for schools, which often have to scramble for pennies and find creative ways to make them last. But from our experience as teachers, leaders, and consultants, we have concluded that leaders can do much to help their schools thrive without breaking the bank. This is not to say these practices are free. They do require an investment: your time.

In the chapters that follow, we offer specific recommendations and practical tools that will help your school develop a healthy culture. In most cases, we are addressing all levels of leadership—central office personnel, school-based administrators, and teacher leaders. Even when the practices are geared more toward a specific group, all staff members can benefit from knowing where their school is headed and how they can support that progress.

We believe that you already have the resources necessary for improvement; we are simply illustrating how to better maximize them. As such, this book is informed by three overarching questions:

- How can your school refine its leadership?
- How can your school maximize teaching and learning to foster growth?
- What changes will enhance a school's efficacy and, consequently, increase achievement?

This book is not a recipe that must be followed to the letter. We encourage you to read ahead and move around as you see fit, according to your school's needs. If you are open to doing things a little differently, the following pages should help you gain a new understanding of the complexities and joys of helping your school thrive.

1

Honing Your Leadership and Growing New Leaders

What Is an Effective Leader?

Imagine that it is a balmy April afternoon, and a long-awaited leadership position has just opened up in your district. In your current school-level leadership position, you have had a positive effect on students and staff. This new position, however, could mark the beginning of the next stage of your career and increase your sphere of influence in improving academic achievement. You weigh the decision of applying for the opening with your mentor, your supervisor, your family, and your friends, all of whom are encouraging. So you draft a cover letter, hone your résumé to highlight your key accomplishments, and practice answering potential interview questions with trusted colleagues.

When the morning of the interview arrives, you put on your most professional attire and take a look in the mirror. There is no doubt that you are the leader they are looking for. You arrive early and, while waiting to be called in to the interview room, examine the district literature on display and mentally rehearse your talking points and questions for the panel. When you are brought in, you radiate warmth and confidence as you shake hands and make eye contact with the panel members. You knowledgeably and convincingly discuss the district's vision, pertinent data, and your educational philosophy. But then the panel asks a question for which you are not quite prepared: "How do you get the most out of your leadership?"

Essentially, what the panel is asking is, What does an effective leader do? This is an important question. Any leader with some level of preparation can parrot buzzwords, share his or her credentials and work history, and describe how he or she efficiently coordinates department or building operations. A leader is expected to do all these things. But an effective leader does more.

Effective leadership is the key to improving academic achievement and attaining lasting change. If you want to help your school thrive, it is a given that what you need to do will hinge on your leadership as well as on those around you. For our purposes, we define leadership as a "process of persuasion or example by which an individual (or leadership team) induces a group to pursue objectives held by the leader or shared by the leader and his or her followers" (Gardner, 1990, p. 1). To reach these objectives, leaders also need to be good managers. Conversely, not all managers are good leaders.

Leadership is a complex, multilayered function essential to any organization's success. A leader's main purpose is to push an organization forward and farther, whereas a manager's primary function is to ensure that the organization operates efficiently.

These two roles have one crucial difference: leaders deal in change, whereas managers deal in stability. Because the current U.S. education climate is focused on accountability, growth, and improvement, effective leadership is particularly important right now. As educational researcher and consultant Robert

Marzano (2003) observes, "Leadership could be considered the single most important aspect of effective school reform" (p. 172). As such, leadership continues to be widely discussed and dissected in educational literature and public forums. Therefore, to hone your own leadership and to grow new leaders, you must first examine what effective leaders do.

Effective Leaders . . .

. . . **Inspire.** Effective leaders inspire those around them. They accomplish this through the vision they set forth, the picture of the future toward which everyone strives. Their passion is contagious, and their energy is evident in everything they approach. Their dedication, commitment, and ability motivate others not just to do as their leaders do but also to believe that what they work toward is within their reach. Effective leaders use themes, mottoes, and symbols to inspire staff members and to maintain their focus on shared objectives.

. . . **Develop Relationships.** Thomas Hoerr (2005) notes that "leadership is about relationships" (p. 7). As much as effective leaders focus on improving instruction, they also invest time in cultivating personal connections. Good leaders listen to staff members and recognize important issues in their lives; they talk with them not just as colleagues but also as people. As a bonus, building these connections uncovers teachers' individual talents and strengths and helps leaders get the most out of their staff.

. . . **Monitor School Climate.** Simply put, effective leaders know what is happening in the building. They are aware of the web of relationships connecting students, staff members, teams, and departments. They stay on top of concerns and complaints connected to school operations. They are conscious of hidden problems, emerging problems, and public problems. Their proactive approach may be as simple as anticipating supply needs and room arrangements or as serious as observing and addressing instructional and personnel issues. Although they must prioritize, they do not minimize any issues' importance to staff members.

. . . **Nurture.** So much of what effective leaders do is nurture others. Wise leaders cultivate their staff members' leadership skills, both to ensure support in carrying out and sustaining change and to establish a network of rising leaders to fill future positions. Effective leaders make sure that no teacher is left behind: they pick up those who have fallen, lend an ear or a shoulder to those who need support, and generally help to recharge staff members and prepare them for another day. Good leaders may not like all of their staff members, but they are sure to demonstrate care and concern for each and every single one of them through their words and actions.

. . . **Set Culture.** Not all leaders have the opportunity to create a culture from scratch; most inherit it from previous leaders. Whether setting a new culture or shifting or enhancing the existing one, however, effective leaders put in place norms and practices—including their choices and methods in hiring, promoting, or not renewing faculty—that ensure productive collaboration, data analysis, staff development, and professional dialogues.

. . . **Maintain Visibility.** When one administrator we know solicited feedback from staff members, the most common observation he heard was that he was not visible enough. He seemed to be around only when things were either really good or really bad. Effective leaders are visible on a regular basis; they are the face of the team, the department, or the school. They are in the halls not only during class changes but also during class, and they find time to talk to teachers and students during lunch and before and after school. Such visibility helps leaders stay in touch with people's needs, wants, and concerns and demonstrates that they are shoulder-to-shoulder alongside their staff in the field.

. . . **Diagnose.** Effective leaders have a keen ability to sense what (or who) isn't working and are able to analyze data to determine what needs to be fixed to improve academic achievement.

They understand the nature of problems as well as their far-reaching effects. They pinpoint problems through effective questioning, and they coordinate plans of action with staff members when appropriate. After diagnosing a problem, effective leaders also discover ways to minimize, sidestep, or eliminate it.

. . . **Celebrate.** Without celebrations, work feels too much like *work*, and things that once felt fun can become onerous. Therefore, effective leaders find reasons to celebrate. They keep morale up by ensuring that victories and gains—no matter how small—are recognized in some form. Verbal or written, personal or public, these celebrations reinforce expectations and help propel staff forward. Effective leaders are creative with how they recognize people, especially if there is no financial support for it. They might provide a special parking space, create a monthly award, or cover a class, but they also know that sometimes the simplest recognition—just thanking someone—can be the best recognition.

. . . **Communicate.** Communication is the foundation of effective leadership. One of the most common staff complaints we hear is that leaders do not communicate in an effective manner. This may mean that they do not communicate expectations clearly or that they disseminate the information too late, causing people to react to it instead of plan for it. Effective leaders eliminate confusion by ensuring in a timely manner and through a variety of methods (such as e-mail, memos, and displays) that staff members are on the same page. These leaders also recognize that communication cuts more than one way: it involves encouraging and listening to feedback from staff.

Say what you mean, and mean what you say.

. . . **Work with Others.** Effective leaders tend to make us feel as though we are working *with* them, not *for* them. They distribute leadership, collaborate with staff, and treat everyone fairly and respectfully. These leaders have a better chance of both accomplishing change and creating a stable environment. Authority is present, but the relationship between staff and leader is collegial, not despotic.

. . . Acknowledge Mistakes. People want to work with someone who is human and fallible—and who does not cover up mistakes or pass the buck. Effective leaders are willing to own up to their mistakes. Doing so does not damage their credibility but actually builds it. Leaders who acknowledge errors demonstrate humility and the fact that they are able and willing to grow and learn from their mistakes. When bottlenecks surface, leaders might be tempted to point the finger at others, but good leaders will first "stop and examine a bottle. Notice where the neck is. It is not at the bottom" (Kline, n.d.). Of course, they must also demonstrate that they will take action to prevent such mistakes from recurring.

. . . Model. When leaders "model the way" (Kouzes & Posner, 2002, p. 14), they lend credibility to their leadership. Effective leaders "take every opportunity to show others by their own example that they're deeply committed to the values and aspirations they espouse. Leading by example is how leaders make visions and values tangible. It's how they provide the *evidence* that they're personally committed" (Kouzes & Posner, 2002, p. 77). Effective leaders demonstrate their willingness to benefit the learning community in any way they can, and they never ask staff members to do something they wouldn't do themselves.

. . . Commit. Effective leaders do what they say they will do, whether they have pledged to a large-scale project or made a minor commitment. This builds credibility and trust among staff members, who realize that their leaders' promises are not empty words. These leaders take on additional responsibilities when necessary, realizing that they may need to sacrifice their own personal desires and work twice as hard as everyone else to fulfill the vision. They demonstrate patience and fully commit to initiatives, not abandoning them midstream if there aren't immediate results.

... **Adjust.** We've known leaders who, when faced with adversity or an unexpected obstacle, are unable to continue with a plan of action. Effective leaders are able to regroup and determine a new course. They understand that needs and goals change over time and are able to adapt to meet them, and they know that sometimes they need to adjust their leadership style to complete a specific task or to work with a particular staff member.

... **Lead.** Although this area seems obvious, it deserves a brief mention nonetheless. Effective leaders initiate and innovate. They have the courage to make decisions, and their actions lead people toward the pursued objective. As former first lady Rosalynn Carter once said, "A leader takes people where they want to go. A great leader takes people where they don't necessarily want to go, but ought to be."

Evaluate and Improve Your Leadership

A question we often ask leaders is, How do you know whether you are effective? Evaluating your own leadership style, and its attendant strengths and weaknesses, is crucial to getting the most out of your leadership. The sections that follow will get you started on the process.

Self-Evaluate

Evaluative instruments such as Myers-Briggs can be useful tools in determining leadership efficacy. They can help us understand our work and leadership styles and often offer tangible results that enable us to work toward self-improvement. However helpful they are, though, these instruments are costly resources that not every school or leader can afford.

An alternative and inexpensive means of self-evaluation is to keep a journal. Simply recording daily interactions and the events leading up to your decisions—and then revisiting them a little later—can provide remarkable objectivity and clarity with regard to your leadership.

> *The unexamined leader is a stagnant leader.*
>
> . . . .

The purpose of journaling is to reflect on what you have done to better understand what you should do in the future. If you are unable to find the time to journal, then set aside some time each day to answer the following questions:

- Did you identify the desired outcome before taking action?
- Was the actual outcome the best possible solution?
- How effective was the method you used in reaching the outcome?
- If it was not effective, what could you have done differently that would have helped you reach a better outcome?
- Are you able to repeat your effective behaviors to get similar future outcomes?
- What are you willing to do differently in the future? What *must* you do differently in the future?
- Who were the others involved, and what were their positions, interests, and stakes?
- What *really* happened, or what was the subtext of the situation or conversation?

While we are in the moment, we are often unaware of how we are thinking, talking, acting, and leading. In our experience, effective leaders find the time to look back on the day's events while simultaneously looking ahead to what they will do in the future. Reflective practitioners "analyze the uniqueness of a problem confronting them, frame the problem in ways that structure its intelligibility, think about the results of their actions, and puzzle out why things worked." These steps help them "build up a reservoir of insights and intuitions that they can call upon as they go about their work" (Starratt, 1995, p. 66).

Survey Staff

A no-cost leadership evaluation approach is to talk to those whom your decisions directly affect. If you feel secure enough to put yourself in this vulnerable position, then surveying your staff is one of the best ways to get meaningful feedback. Just be ready to discuss and respond to their comments. If you don't want to seriously consider the feedback, then don't bother asking for it in the first place.

Bring out the best in your leadership skills by asking your staff what you can do differently to be the leader they need.

. . . .

If you implement a department- or schoolwide survey, make sure that participants are able to respond anonymously (see Resource 2). Although we would all like to know who thinks what, respondents are less likely to be honest if they have to put their names on the survey. We recommend distributing one survey to each staff member's mailbox. Each respondent then returns his or her survey to an "objective observer," such as a secretary, who crosses off the staff member's name on the roster to ensure that people participate only once. This objective observer would then be responsible for pulling all the responses together for your review.

As helpful as surveys can be, some find them a little stifling; teachers are only able to share what they are *asked* to share. So sometimes a more open-ended approach can be helpful. At your next department or faculty meeting, designate an objective observer to pass out sticky notes. Once you have left the room, the objective observer can say to the assem-

Accepting criticism is only part of being a good leader; if you hope to be effective, you must act on it as well.

. . . .

bled staff members, "Use the sticky note in front of you to record what you would like to tell our supervisor." This anonymous process encourages staff members to share what is important to them—often things that might not have appeared on a survey. Consider some of the responses we have collected on school visits:

- "I wish you weren't always so rude in the morning."
- "I love how you always seem to know when to ask how I'm doing."
- "How come it seems like you never say 'hi' to me when we pass each other in the hall?"

Identify a Game Plan

Seeking and receiving feedback is one thing; acting on it is something else altogether. Once you receive this information, you will probably feel overwhelmed. You might have already guessed at some areas that need improvement, but there will likely be areas that catch you off guard. You should pay special attention to these; if other people are seeing behaviors or actions of which you are unaware, you might want to engage in some careful, honest introspection and consider addressing these areas first.

Categorize Your Improvement

Sometimes it seems like the best way to accomplish anything in life is simply to make a list. And that is exactly what we recommend in this case. Choose three goals for improvement over the course of a year—one categorized as easy, one short-term, and one long-term.

The easy goal should be something that is a quick win, reached relatively easily and visibly. This kind of goal is important because it is a gesture to staff that you are serious in your improvement efforts. For example, administrators at Falls Church High School in Virginia responded to students' concern that they did not have sufficient input by selecting an unused locker away from the main office, painting it red, and encouraging students to submit their thoughts on slips of paper through the vents.

A short-term goal is one that you would work on over the course of a marking period (nine weeks) or so and that requires more contemplation and planning. For example, one administrator we know received complaints from teachers that he was not visible enough in the school. He began scheduling time into his calendar to be visible during class changes in different parts of the building as well as during instructional periods.

The long-term goal involves more work and bigger changes, but its payoff will benefit all. For example, a colleague of ours sets a goal called "Flip Five." His goal is to identify five teachers with leadership potential and, over the course of a year or two, mentor them and set them on the path of a leadership career as teacher leaders or administrators.

Share Your Plan

Verbalizing your intentions to others not only provides you with support from colleagues but also keeps you accountable and demonstrates an open and sincere desire to improve. If you fail to do what you say you will, you run the risk of being seen as insincere.

Keep It Fresh and Alive

Once you have identified your goals and plan of action, you should keep them at the forefront of your mind. Continually check your actions against your game plan to see if they fit. If so, pat yourself on the back; if not, make adjustments either to your game plan or to your actions.

It is also helpful to post goals where you will see them daily—at home, in your car, or in your office, for example—just as you might with personal goals. You could even write your goals as pop-up messages that greet you when you turn on your computer.

Finally, just as you do for your staff members, keep up your morale and motivation by celebrating your victories and milestones.

Share the Responsibility of Leadership

As a school leader, you will only be as strong and effective as those who surround and support you. Too many leaders succumb to the lure of being a lone visionary or hero.

Some adopt this leadership style because it is how they were trained or "how things have always been done." Many subscribe to an antiquated notion that they must be the sole source of decision making and change in the building.

Unfortunately, maintaining a power monopoly of top-down leadership will not lead to much improvement because, quite simply, people don't like being told what to do. Most teachers want to share in the responsibility of decision making. When you welcome this kind of participation, you confirm that you value your teachers and their contributions.

Leaders who try to effect change single-handedly are often accused of being autocratic or dictatorial, or of being out of touch with the faculty and its needs and challenges. And in these schools, the leadership positions that do exist are usually filled with managers who merely perform the daily operations needed to maintain a team, grade level, or department. Their skills and potential remain largely untapped.

Distribution of leadership is crucial. Leaders cannot be everything to everybody all the time. When they attempt to, they only overwhelm themselves and others. Teachers "cannot expect much from a leader mired in chores that should have been left to well-chosen teammates" (Gardner, 1990, p. 150), and when these responsibilities are not distributed, the leader's efficacy is severely diminished.

Effective leaders know where they need to go, but they also know that they must invite others to assist in the journey.

As Gardner (1990) notes, "No leader has all the skills—and certainly not the time—to carry out all the complex tasks of contemporary leadership" (p. 10). The various demands and stresses of leadership can fatigue even the most effective leaders at times. Marzano, Waters, and McNulty (2005) further point out that "leading a school requires a complex array of skills. . . . It would be rare, indeed, to find a single individual who has the capacity or will to master such a complex array of skills. How does one reconcile the fact that effective school leadership requires 21 responsibilities but that the mastery of all 21 is beyond the capacity of most people?" (p. 99).

Education leaders can increase their efficacy by creating shared leadership teams that make strategic use of staff members' special skills. Marzano (2003) defines a shared leadership team as "the principal and other administrators operating as key players working with a dedicated group of classroom teachers" (p. 175). Such teams build a strong support system that moves the school forward more easily than a single leader can. The following sections will help you get started.

Create a Shared Leadership Team

Creating a shared leadership team is an important first step toward neutralizing the problems of a vertical leadership structure. The team is composed of "people with complementary skills who are committed to a common purpose, performance goals, and common approach for which they hold themselves accountable" (Katzenbach & Smith, 1993, p. 111). As active learners, the members of the team are "highly committed to the general well-being of the school. Members share a 'culture of commitment' regarding the school" (Marzano et al., 2005, p. 104).

Ideally, this collection of administrators and teacher leaders meets at least once a month to identify academic areas in need of improvement and to initiate and implement strategies to improve student achievement. The leadership team is not a vehicle for the micromanagement of the school; rather, it is the driving force behind change and a necessary component in ensuring the school's success. In most cases, the team's discussions and activities should be replicated in the members' grade-level, team, or department meetings, an example of turnaround training.

If your school has no leadership team, you can increase capacity by assembling a leadership team of administrators, department chairs, and team leaders.

You can choose any name that fits your team's stated purpose— for example, the Instructional Council, the School Leadership

Team, or the Instructional Leadership Team. If you plan to change the team's responsibilities from previous years or are otherwise planning to give the team a fresh start, you may want to change the current name. It can be interesting to hear how staff members who are not team members think of these teams. Staff members who can't see a clearly defined purpose or measurable results will probably view the leadership team as a club of the privileged few who have little impact on their daily professional lives. Thus, an effective team earns staff respect by clearly articulating its vision and purpose throughout the school.

Leadership team meetings should focus on instruction, assessment, and other areas related to academic achievement. Anything else is extraneous. To ensure that the team's practices and processes are transparent, a participant should record minutes of the meeting. After team members have reviewed and accepted the minutes, they can share the notes with the rest of the school (with the exception of more private or sensitive information) by putting them on a network directory or in a public folder. If this technology is not available in your building, print and distribute the notes to the staff or have them housed in a convenient, central location, such as where teacher mailboxes are kept. You will find that sharing minutes will build respect and trust for the leadership team and its purpose.

Change people by modeling the desired behaviors. Recording and distributing notes from meetings is one easy example.

Engage and Involve the Right People

Jim Collins (2001) has informed us that "the old adage 'people are our greatest asset' turns out to be wrong. People are *not* your greatest asset. The *right* people are" (p. 13). He urges leaders to make sure that the right people are "on the bus" (p. 41). To achieve sustainable success, you must have the right people in the right leadership positions. Not every leader can build a team from scratch, however. If you are working with a preexisting leadership team, you might have inherited some passengers, to continue Collins's metaphor. You then need to determine who is on the bus, who should be on the bus, and how to get others to disembark at the next stop if need be.

If your school already has a shared leadership team, take a careful inventory of the membership. You need to identify key players, supporters, and detractors. Begin by asking yourself the following questions:

- Who are the team members?
- Why are they considered leaders?
- Are they considered leaders just because of their positions or titles?
- How were they originally given leadership positions? Based on what criteria?
- Do they really lead and have followers, or do they just belong to a team and possess a leadership title? If they don't have followers, how can they lead?
- Have they reached their leadership capacity? If so, is that a detriment to the team?

The "powerhouse" of the leadership team can be found in two tiers. Tier one includes

- The principal.
- The assistant principal(s).
- The athletic director.
- The staff development coordinator.
- The guidance director/lead counselor.
- The dean of students.
- The administrative intern.
- The school resource officer.

Tier two includes

- Department chairs.
- Team leaders.
- Lead teachers.
- The instructional coach.
- The technology specialist.
- A guidance counselor.
- The activities coordinator.
- Aspiring teacher leaders.

Although your leadership team does not need to mirror this template exactly, these people form the base of the decision makers in your school, with the exception of the school resource officer (SRO). SROs are local law enforcement agents who serve as liaisons between schools and the police. They establish a presence in schools to deter infractions and criminal behavior, forge relationships with students and staff, and actively work with school leaders to ensure a safe learning environment for students and staff. Because SROs can have a direct influence on the quality of instruction, we recommend that they participate in meetings, although they are not voting members of the leadership team and should not be expected to remain for the meetings' entire duration. If your school has a safety specialist, then it would also be wise to extend to him or her the responsibility of attendance.

We break the leadership team into two tiers because there will be times when it is necessary or desirable to assemble only the first tier. Overall, however, the two tiers should work in conjunction. The members of this team act as leaders of the leader: they will help you monitor the pulse of your school's culture, strengthen your leadership through ownership, and advise on and implement change.

Surround Yourself with Those Who Are Better Than You

Teachers sometimes feel threatened by their neighboring classroom teachers, especially when those neighbors excel. This feeling of threat is one of the principal causes of teacher isolation. Often, the situation is no different for leaders.

We have been in too many schools that have a good principal but mediocre supporting leadership. This deficit could be due to a lack of training and coaching, but many principals actually prefer this situation because it safely preserves their ego and pride. If the principal is strong, this situation may not have a particularly negative effect on the team's or the school's overall efficacy. But what if the school has a mediocre principal? Consider how difficult it will be just to maintain school affairs, much less provide strong leadership. As John Gardner (1990) notes, leaders should choose high-caliber colleagues, but "all too often they recruit individuals who have as their prime qualities an unswerving loyalty to the boss" (p. 150). Gardner further explains that "what might have been a leadership team becomes, all too often, a rule clique or circle of sycophants" (p. 150). Although loyalty is admirable, it should hardly be the top consideration in making hiring decisions.

When we discuss leaders surrounding themselves with equally strong (or stronger) leaders, we can't help but think of Joe Torre, the highly successful former manager of the New York Yankees, who captured a World Series title in his first year at their helm. During the 2006 baseball season in particular, he found himself working with one of the most talented coaching staffs ever assembled.

Effective leaders are secure leaders.

Each of the coaches—from the bench coach to the pitching coach—could easily have been the manager for another professional team. Instead, they chose to work with Torre. In return, Torre, never threatened by the immense talent that surrounded him, shared his leadership with his coaching staff. Relying on the coaches' input and instincts, Torre guided the team to success during an injury-plagued season. His distribution of leadership and professionalism over the years helped him bring out the best in his coaches and in his team. An insightful, decisive leader who demonstrated an uncanny knack for making the right decisions, he will be remembered as one of the most successful managers in baseball history. Principals also have the potential to be remembered as effective leaders if they display the same courage and build a cadre of strong leaders to work with.

Consider Having Leaders Reapply for Their Positions

This is a strategy that should be used only in extreme cases. Although an ill school culture or ineffective leaders may make it necessary for you to consider this option, you should keep in mind that it could have a detrimental effect on morale and climate. We know one principal who saw the need to eliminate complacency in his large suburban school, so he removed all teachers from their leadership positions and asked them to reapply. Although he was correct in assessing that something needed to change, this drastic move caused already-low staff morale to plummet even further.

That said, you should not necessarily steer away from this option. You are doing this for other teachers, not for yourself, so some staff members might even appreciate such action. Starting from scratch might be necessary; you just need to find a way to sell it to the rest of the staff. You might consider addressing your intentions at a faculty meeting as a means of fostering leadership growth, especially if you have leaders who have held their positions for a number of years.

More selling and less telling of new strategies will win buy-in.

You might explain that people who sit in leadership positions for too long may be unwittingly inhibiting others' professional growth. Finally, if you do have just one or two leaders whom you would like to replace, this process helps you avoid accusations of bias.

Identify Expectations for Your Leaders

Your school's shared leadership team plays a pivotal role in effecting powerful, sustainable change. You should have high expectations of your leaders. The members of the leadership team are responsible for monitoring and adjusting their departments' or teams' instructional programs; for articulating these instructional programs to students and parents; for assisting in the selection of teachers and team members; for coaching teachers; for serving as liaisons between their teachers and the subject coordinators and administrators; and for managing allocated resources.

We have drawn on our extensive experiences in numerous schools to define and describe five main leadership areas for teacher leaders. The following sections will clarify expectations for anyone in a leadership role, including you to some extent. Because teacher leaders and leadership team members are sometimes unsure of what their positions entail, each section contains a bulleted list of expectations that can serve as a guide and an evaluative tool. Of course, you should discuss these items with your team members before adopting them as leadership standards for your school. You will notice that there is some overlap among the items in the different sections because seldom do leadership duties fit into tidy little boxes.

If you talk the talk and expect others to walk that talk, be sure to be willing to lead the way.

Instructional Leadership

One of the main responsibilities of team members, instructional leadership is key in improving academic achievement. Although this role does have some managerial aspects, knowledge of instructional strategies, current research, and literature as well as the ability to apply data are imperative. Leadership team members

- Serve on the shared leadership team.

- Assume a main role in the development of their respective subject areas' school improvement plan.

- Meet periodically with the principal and the area supervisor of instruction to discuss program and instructional matters.

- Establish vision and direction for their respective departments.

- Coordinate school-level diagnostic pre-tests and post-tests.

- Mine and use assessment data to develop goals and action plans for their departments.

- Hold departmental meetings to discuss instructional concerns of their departments and the school.

- Initiate and/or guide curriculum mapping.

- Seek ways to involve students meaningfully in their education program.

- Adapt the county program to the needs of the local school community.

- Help plan the best program for each instructional group by adapting the curriculum to the needs of the individuals.

- Review department members' midterm and final examinations for consistency and rigor and provide constructive feedback.

- Work with the department, the administration, the guidance department, and other academic and support departments in developing the schedule and placing students in appropriate classes.

- Assist classroom teachers in classroom organization and management; in locating, selecting, and securing instructional materials; and in interpreting test results to assess each student's abilities and performance.

- Conduct self-evaluation, self-improvement, and evaluation of programs.

- Develop plans for daily work as well as long-range planning.
- Plan for the most productive use of paraprofessionals, aides, and volunteers.

You should meet regularly with your instructional leaders to

- Help them identify powerful instructional strategies and effective elements of lesson plans.
- Share what you look for when you conduct classroom observations.
- Discuss how assessments should look, how often teachers should be assessing students, and how assessments should be weighted.
- Discuss how they can support novice teachers by observing them, having them observe other teachers, demonstrating instructional strategies for them, and providing opportunities for them to practice these techniques.

Professional Development

Just as you help your teacher leaders grow, they in turn must help their teachers grow. Establishing goals and long-range plans and promoting professional development are essential responsibilities of any leader. Leadership team members

- Help plan staff development activities.
- Develop departmental goals that are consistent with school, school system, and county goals.
- Adjust programs as necessary to meet changing demands.
- Assist teachers in developing long-range plans.
- Develop a professional library or set of resources for their respective departments.
- Help interview and select prospective teachers for their departments.
- Stimulate an awareness of research and curriculum development in their subject areas.

- Help teachers identify the most effective ways of using courses of study and instructional materials.
- Play a key role in matching new teachers to mentors.
- Keep informed of new trends and programs in their fields of responsibility.
- Participate in inservice activities related to their duties.
- Act as members of relevant review and evaluation committees.
- Assist in writing curriculum materials.
- Confer frequently with members of their departments on an informal basis.

To help your leaders develop their programs and promote teachers' professional growth, you should

- Look at standardized test data with your leaders to see where their teams or departments are excelling and where they are falling short with certain objectives or strands.
- Help them brainstorm staff development sessions for their departments that would address problem areas.
- Assist in designing "getting to know you" activities for mentors and their mentees as well as mini-workshops for the novice teachers that address classroom management, building responsibilities, and lesson plans.

Departmental Administration

This area is more managerial in nature than the other areas, but effectively carrying out administrative and clerical functions is an important part of leadership. Organizational skills and the ability to complete tasks and meet deadlines in a timely fashion are crucial. Leadership team members

- Assist the principal in providing overall leadership and management of the school's instructional program.

- Provide the school's leadership with meeting agendas and minutes.
- Monitor and make use of data pertinent to student achievement.
- Coordinate departmental housekeeping and clerical duties.
- Align the culture of their respective departments with the school culture set by the principal.
- Lead departmental team-building activities.
- Foster cooperative interpersonal relationships within the department.
- Keep classroom teachers informed on local school matters.
- Coordinate the use and maintain the care of equipment and materials.
- Supervise the use of the clerical and instructional aides assigned to the department.
- Greet, orient, and monitor substitute teachers, providing support as needed.
- Arrange emergency class coverage when necessary.
- Pre-approve all departmental transactions (e.g., purchase orders, teacher leave, guest speakers, field trips, and requests for auditorium use).

To support your leaders in this area, you should

- Discuss with your leaders what makes meetings effective or ineffective and talk about how to facilitate a meeting; most teacher leaders have never received training or guidance in this area.
- Share practices that will help them increase their departments' productivity, such as creating an agenda, taking minutes, and identifying leadership roles present in their departmental meetings.

- Introduce them to team-building activities to use throughout the year to develop trust and improve climate.
- Show them the school's master calendar and explain how their departments' instructional programs fit in with the overall operations of the school.

Liaison Function

Communicating concerns and expectations and relaying information to pertinent and vested parties are a crucial part of leadership. As a liaison, leadership team members

- Meet with the principal and the director of instruction to share and discuss concerns related to their instructional programs.
- Keep the school administration and the relevant area and county supervisors informed on departmental matters of curriculum and instruction.
- Join team and department members in parent conferences when appropriate.
- Meet regularly with subject supervisors.

Your responsibilities to your liaisons are to

- Coach your leaders on how to mediate and interact in a parent conference, especially if it involves a complaint about one of their teachers.
- Stress to them the importance of timely communication.
- Share examples of memos for communication and documentation purposes.
- Advise them on the most effective ways to communicate information to department members while not overloading them.

Professionalism

Leadership team members must lead by example. Their scope of professionalism is not limited to what happens in front of the chalkboard; the way they conduct themselves in carrying out their duties and in interacting with colleagues is also important. Leadership team members

- Model expectations and appropriate behavior for department members.
- Arrive punctually to work and meetings.
- Display a professional appearance.
- Communicate in a professional manner.
- Forge and maintain collegial relationships across the school.
- Fulfill obligations and responsibilities in an effective and expeditious manner.

To help your leaders grow professionally, you should

- Share time management tips and explain ways you prioritize and juggle tasks.
- Attend meetings led by your leaders and meet with them afterward to discuss their verbal and nonverbal interactions and communication with their staff.
- Invite them to accompany you to functions where you demonstrate how you connect and interact with different people in different positions.

Help Your Leaders Meet Expectations

The descriptions of these five leadership areas will help your teacher leaders understand what you expect of them. In addition, they provide you with rich material to help your teacher leaders excel. Consider using regular leadership team meetings as job-

Solicit input and agreement on your school's leadership team standards, then clearly and consistently communicate and enforce the expectations.

. . . .

embedded professional development opportunities. If you set aside time at each meeting to focus on certain areas, you will nurture leadership while modeling expectations for what should happen in department and team meetings.

For these sessions, consider pulling articles related to some of the expectations for the team to review and discuss. You might model some of the expectations and provide examples or conduct activities pertaining to them. You could also enlist the help of your leaders in providing training. For example, for the instructional leadership expectation of "mining and using assessment data to develop goals and action plans for the department," a knowledgeable team member could teach the rest of the team how to "slice" and apply data in this way. These members would then be able to train the staff in their departments and grade-level teams on how to use data, set goals, and create plans based on those goals.

Make Good Use of Your Leaders

As we mentioned earlier, leaders cannot be everything to everyone all the time. You should rely on your teacher leaders to help you whenever possible. In the following three sections, we describe ways your teacher leaders can take ownership of supporting your school's mission and fostering academic achievement.

Conducting Curriculum Reviews

Good leaders don't just influence people; they monitor them as well. Mike Schmoker (2006) recommends that "principals and teacher leaders meet with teacher teams by month or quarter to review and discuss evidence of what is actually being taught" (p. 130).

Simply mapping out curriculum is not enough. Even with maps or sequence guides provided by district-level offices and textbook companies, there is still a good chance that teams and departments display a bit of what Kim Marshall calls "curriculum anarchy" (2003). As much as we encourage teachers to collaborate with one another, the bottom line is that once the bell rings, they are alone in their classrooms and able to teach whatever they like. Other than a couple of classroom visits each year, administrators don't have a full picture of what is actually going on. This "'don't ask, don't tell' culture" (2006, p. 130), as Schmoker calls it, is common in most schools, departments, and teams.

The notion of monitoring instruction and curriculum coverage may greatly disturb some teachers; they will exclaim, "We're professionals, so we should be trusted to do our jobs right!" And they are correct. However, the stark reality is that today's stakes are high. Conducting curriculum reviews is an important way to "ensure that standards are actually *taught*" (Schmoker, 2006, p. 131). As Schmoker argues, "In many schools, such reviews would have more impact than all the initiatives we have ever launched, combined. . . . Until such reviews (or some tough-minded equivalent) become as common as school desks, there is no sense in expecting serious improvements in teaching and learning" (p. 130). Leadership team members should conduct these reviews quarterly, meeting with their respective teams and departments to review evidence that teachers are delivering the approved curriculum. Whereas most leaders focus on data (results), curriculum reviews force them to examine delivery and content (process). Your leadership team members are your content experts, so they are the natural ones to conduct these reviews.

Therefore, during the curriculum reviews, team or department members should bring not just test results and other data but also lesson plans, projects, and assessments. The teacher leaders should ask such questions as, "How did your students fare on this assignment, and why do you think that is?" and "How do

How do you know your teachers are regularly teaching and doing what is best for students?

. . . .

you think this lesson or unit went?" (See Resource 3.) Leadership team members should review grade books and lesson plans, but they also need to reassure teachers that these reviews are neither punitive nor evaluative in nature (although they could be used as evidence to support an unsatisfactory evaluation of a consistently underperforming teacher). Although the obvious purpose of these reviews is to monitor what is occurring in teachers' classrooms, the reviews also provide struggling teachers with opportunities for collaboration and support.

Then, at leadership team meetings, teacher leaders can discuss issues from the curriculum reviews, assess their teams' progress, brainstorm ways to refine the curriculum review process, and keep the administration updated on what is occurring throughout the building. Some might view this as micromanagement, but it is not. The leadership team and the administration are not telling teachers what to do; the curriculum guides determine that. Rather, they are simply ensuring that *the right things are being done*.

Performing Classroom Observations

Again, because your leadership team members are your instruction and content experts, you should tap into their knowledge base by having them perform classroom observations. In some schools, teachers are not used to being observed by teacher leaders, so they might demonstrate some initial resistance to this idea. However, if you and your teacher leaders clearly explain that these observations are not in lieu of the formal observations that make up their evaluations, you should be able to allay their concerns.

These observations indeed won't formally be factored into evaluations, but they will be another source of information for you. They offer a cost-effective way of having another set of eyes and ears observing what is occurring in your school's classrooms, and they provide another resource for teachers who might need assistance.

Bringing Solutions

If a single leader cannot perform all the complex tasks necessary to lead a school, then he or she certainly won't be able to solve the plethora of problems that inevitably rise up alone. Instead, you should encourage and even require your leaders to actively engage in problem solving. Leaders should expect team members to bring not just their problems to the table but also their *solutions*, even if they aren't always viable.

You can also demonstrate your faith and trust in your leaders by bringing your own problems to the team. Together, the team members bring a variety of leadership styles and strengths to the table, making the collaborative problem-solving process that much more effective.

Your Responsibilities to Your Leaders

As a leader, you have responsibilities to students and staff to maintain the health of the school and its culture. But you also have responsibilities to your leaders—your current ones as well as your future ones. Specifically, you need to ensure that building leaders are adhering to expectations and make sure that you have a pool of future leaders to draw from.

Enforce Expectations

As we mentioned before, you can use the five leadership areas we described to make your expectations and values clear. If one of your leadership team members is not fully meeting expectations, you need to have a professional conversation with that leader. For example, say one of your teacher leaders demonstrates a lack of professionalism by routinely arriving late for work and meetings. This leader is conveying the message that her time is more important than the team's time and that she is not accountable to expectations.

We have seen how this kind of behavior, left unaddressed, can erode respect for teacher leadership and, by extension, the school's leadership. Therefore, we recommend opening a dialogue with something along these lines: "Natalie, I notice you have not been arriving to school on time. You know that is not consistent with being a leader in this building, and you know you are expected to be a role model for the others. I feel confident that you can fix this. Would you agree?"

How can she respond? If she says "yes" and is able to rectify the behavior, then the team benefits. If she says "no," then she is admitting not the failures but her inability to rectify them, which implies that she needs help in doing so. In fact, it almost sounds as though she is asking you to place her on a work plan for improvement if the behavior continues. (See Resource 4.) If the behavior continues, we recommend formal documentation that includes your efforts to support her and to clarify behavior and performance expectations. If she is unable or unwilling to change her behavior, then you have already initiated a dialogue on why she should not return in a leadership capacity.

The above approach works because you are ultimately affirming your leader's ability to rectify a problem. However, sometimes a conversation is not enough. If your leader does not consistently meet expectations, you need to explicitly state the disconnect between the expectations and the behavior and then outline a more formal plan. Offer some support, such as having him or her observe more effective leaders. Confer with your leader regularly about his or her progress (or lack thereof), and be sure to document your efforts to help. You should also document ways in which your leader continues to fall short to prepare for the worst-case scenario of removing him or her from the leadership position.

Develop Leadership Capacity

As a school leader, one of your main responsibilities is developing the leadership capacity of others. In *On Leadership*, Gardner (1990) relates a conversation he had with the chair of a well-known corporation. This executive bemoaned the fact that the industry's culture rewarded people for "keeping their noses to the grindstones, doing their narrow jobs unquestioningly. Then when a top post opens up, we look around in frustration and say, 'Where are the statesmen?' No one consciously intended to eliminate statesmen; but the organizational culture produced that result" (p. 173). Schools are no different.

Schools often fail to produce "statesmen" because administrators tend to focus energy and resources on enhancing teachers' instructional practices rather than their leadership abilities. Admirable and necessary as it is to improve what occurs inside classrooms, however, school leaders need to pay equal attention to what teachers can be doing outside them. Too often, schools have no plan for filling future leadership vacancies other than pulling up the applicant database. This lack of a plan might not be purposeful; rather, leaders are just happy to have good teachers in their classrooms so they can focus their energy and attention elsewhere. But the better your leaders and teachers, the greater the chance that they will eventually move up in the leadership hierarchy and/or leave the school.

Mentor a Potential Leader

We hope that you are able to identify a person who was instrumental in your career, someone who encouraged you on your path toward leadership. This person might have spotted something in you that no one else had seen before and taken an active role in your development. Maybe he or she provided guidance and support to you along the way, listening to you and building you up when you needed it most. Unfortunately, mentoring potential leaders is not a norm in most schools. Yet mentoring a staff member who has leadership aspirations—what we call "growing a leader"— is an effective way to get the most out of your (future) leaders.

Mentoring a potential leader is a time commitment on the part of both mentor and mentee, so you should be sure to identify someone who is interested in developing this kind of relationship.

You should meet regularly with your mentee. Ideally, you should dedicate 30 minutes a week. We know that might be a considerable time commitment, but as the relationship progresses, the mentee will invariably encounter situations that he or she will want to discuss as soon as possible. If you delay the conference by a week or two, you run the risk of losing a "teachable moment" and the mentee's excitement.

One of the best strategies you have at your disposal is simply sharing stories. Yours are a valuable source of information, so we encourage you to relate leadership anecdotes. Once you have built up a level of trust, you can share with your mentee how you have addressed situations with difficult parents, difficult students, and even difficult teachers, and your decision-making process along the way. As your relationship progresses, encourage your mentee to share his or her own stories about handling difficult situations. Coach your mentee by asking probing, open-ended questions about how else he or she might handle scenarios while enlarging his or her view of the school and how its different areas are interconnected.

When you meet with your mentee, you are not necessarily there to evaluate or judge; you are there to build up his or her skills and confidence. On occasions when you must be critical, try to make sure that your mentee leaves the meeting feeling good about his or her potential and excited about pursuing the leadership path. You should also encourage your mentee to take on new challenges and get outside his or her comfort zone. Finally, help him or her build networks with other potential leaders as well as official leaders inside the building, in other schools, and at the central office.

Groom a Backup

Potential leaders learn by doing. It's a good idea for administrators to groom their teacher leaders to serve in their absence and for teacher leaders to coach their teachers to lead in their absence. In this way, the principal, assistant principals, department chairs, and team leaders all have backups to act on their behalf. According to Gardner (1990), this practice activates "widening circles of supplementary leadership. Such an extended network reaching out from the leadership center carries messages both ways. It can be equally effective in letting the intentions of leadership be known or in tapping a broad range of advice and advocacy" (p. 151). In addition, providing teachers with new challenges helps stem job stagnation and turnover.

We recommend that you set up some learning opportunities for your teacher leaders during their planning periods. They could observe you handling discipline issues or meeting with a parent, for example. Follow up these observations with a discussion on choices you made, words you used, and nonverbal behavior you employed. Once you believe your backup has soaked up enough information, assign him or her some minor responsibilities and follow up with further discussion and reflection.

When you're comfortable with having your backup act independently, have him or her fill in on your behalf the next time you are absent. Leave a "lesson plan," just as a classroom teacher would for a substitute teacher. If you are an assistant principal, for example, leave a list of referrals to address student discipline issues. You could also request that your backup conduct a teacher observation (which of course wouldn't go in the teacher's file) or "5 × 5's"—five five-minute drop-in visits to classes outside his or her department. This will broaden the substitute's knowledge of how the different areas of the school function. You could have your backup draft a memo to the staff, develop an agenda for or facilitate a leadership team meeting, or organize an event to further build his or her skills. Department chairs and team leaders should have similar expectations for teachers they are coaching if they will be out. Be sure to have a post-conference with your backup soon after you return to discuss his or her experiences and provide constructive feedback and guidance.

Above all else, you must put your backups to work; the last thing you want to communicate is that you don't have much to do. If they are aspiring to a higher step on the leadership ladder, then it is your responsibility to provide realistic experiences for your substitutes. At the same time, you don't want them to think that your job is impossible to manage, which could dampen their aspirations.

Transform Informal Leaders into "Official" Leaders

Another way to cultivate leadership and foster staff ownership and buy-in is to tap the potential of the "informal leaders" in the school. These aren't the department chairs or the team leaders, yet people still look to them for leadership and trust their judgment. You could have them sit on the kind of leadership team often referred to as a Faculty Advisory Committee, a Faculty Team, or a School Issues Team. Their duties, among others, might involve collecting staff concerns related to operational, facility, safety, and building matters and bringing them to the principal for discussion and resolution.

If you want to avoid the perception that you are handpicking certain staff members to lead the school, then you might want to consider implementing an anonymous voting process, which would most likely still elect the informal leaders you are targeting while conveying trust and demonstrating that leadership, while not always democratic, can be participative. You can replicate the process to fill other leadership positions, such as the chair of the School Climate Team and so on.

Making a Difference

To get the most out of your leadership, you need to muster all the courage you can in the face of today's accountability pressures. It takes courage to decide to make a difference, to put yourself on the line and give harder and more than others. Let the courage of your convictions inspire and motivate others, and then fulfill your leadership responsibility by growing new leaders. There are no excuses for not doing so. Nothing that we have advocated here has a financial impact, and investing the time to develop others should be a categorical imperative for leaders. Leadership can no longer be the responsibility of the few. Once your leaders are in place and seasoned, you are well on your way toward helping your school thrive. And with the leadership network you build, the goal of establishing your learning community's vision and mission, as we discuss in the following chapter, becomes that much easier.

Getting Started

- Identify areas of your leadership that need improvement, and create a plan to achieve your goals.

- Assemble a shared leadership team. If one already exists, refine its purpose and expectations.

- Develop the leadership potential of staff members, and provide job-embedded staff development to help them grow.

- Expand the responsibilities and authority of leaders in the school.

2

Developing a Vision and a Mission

Imagine that you have a rare weekend without any professional responsibilities: no papers to grade, no lessons to plan, no activities to cover. To take advantage of this unexpected free time, you and three friends decide to go on a fishing excursion to a lake known as one of the best largemouth bass habitats in the eastern United States. Through e-mail messages, telephone conversations, and brief get-togethers, the four of you coordinate transportation, lodging, the time of departure, and other details.

It would seem reasonable to assume that you were all going with ambitions to catch largemouth bass. However, what would happen to the trip's camaraderie and outcome if each person's vision of the weekend differed from that assumption? What if one person plans to spot eagles, another is looking for lakefront property, and a third hopes to catch anything that will pull on the line, while you are there for sun and leisure?

You could have avoided any confusion and better harnessed efforts by explicitly asking your companions during the planning stages,

- What is the actual purpose of the trip?
- What are the goals of the attendees?
- What does everyone envision for the weekend?
- Has everyone shared these things with one another?

Whatever the context, the point is the same: if a group wants to move forward, it needs to develop an understood, agreed-on purpose. With a couple of word substitutions, you could ask those bulleted questions of any leadership team or department in your school. If the team has a healthy culture, its members would likely give similar answers.

Stopping to confirm common goals among the stakeholders will help the team meet its objectives.

Developing strong vision and mission statements can help stakeholders in your school reach such a common understanding. A vision is your school's goal—where you hope to see it in the future. The mission provides an overview of the steps planned to achieve that future. A vision is concise and easy to recall, whereas a mission is lengthier and more explanatory in nature. Your school may also want to establish targets along the way to measure progress toward its vision. We begin this chapter with developing your school's vision, because you need to know where you want to be before you can determine how you plan to get there.

Drafting the Vision Statement

According to the Task Force on Developing Research in Educational Leadership (2003), "Effective educational leaders help their schools to develop or endorse visions that embody the best thinking about teaching and learning. School leaders inspire others to reach for ambitious goals" (p. 3). Your school must have a vision that all staff members recognize as a common direction of growth, something that inspires them to be better. An effective vision also announces to parents and students where you are heading and why they should take the trip with you.

One of the most important responsibilities of any leader is establishing a vision and inviting others to share in its development.

Without a vision, your school lacks direction. As the ancient Roman philosopher Seneca observed, "If a man knows not what harbor he seeks, any wind is the right wind." If you don't have a common, agreed-on destination, then everyone is left to his or her own devices to imagine one—a scenario that results in unharnessed and unfocused efforts, with everyone believing that what he or she is doing is right. A common understanding of the destination allows all stakeholders to align their improvement efforts. And the best part of planning for this journey is that it doesn't cost anything to decide where you want to go.

As important as the vision is, we have found that keeping it alive throughout the year is not an easy task. For you to get the most out of your vision, you must first remove the barriers from making it an integral, vibrant facet of the school community.

Eliminate Obstacles

One of the first obstacles that will come up is people's fear of change. Creating or adjusting a vision statement is an unmistakable indicator of imminent change. It is helpful to have an idea of the internal dialogues your staff members will likely be having before, during, and even after the development of the new vision. (This also applies to the development of a new mission.) Listening to and validating staff members' thoughts will help them cope with the change as they ask themselves the following questions:

- What is the need for a new vision?
- Will I be able to live with the new vision?
- Will I be able to support the new vision?
- What will the new vision expect of me?
- How will my world change as a result?
- Will I be able to continue doing what I've always done? Why or why not?
- Do I believe in this new vision?
- Do I believe in my school's ability to achieve this vision?
- Do I believe I can help make the vision happen?

Another potential obstacle to creating a powerful vision is the reality that vision statements are often created perfunctorily and lack follow-through. They are usually the result of a directive to "get it done" by a certain date and delivered to a central office supervisor.

Such directives often lead to vision statements that have been created in a rush by one person or by a small group of individuals with no input from other stakeholders. Such statements are rarely understood or acknowledged by others in the school, and who can blame them? The process precludes genuine buy-in. Although school leadership must have a vision for the future, it should be used as a way to open up a dialogue rather than be handed down from on high.

Don't rush the vision statement; doing so leads to skepticism, stress, and distrust, which will lead to a statement that will eventually be ignored.

Because these closed approaches to developing vision statements are incredibly common, most staff members are turned off by the mere mention of the words *vision* and *mission* and groan at the prospect of yet another initiative that will eventually be forgotten—that after a flurry of activity, the vision will be shelved alongside the school improvement plan, out of the reach and off the minds of staff members. Because they had little involvement in it, they see no real reason to dedicate themselves to it. If setbacks occur along the way, most will shrug their shoulders because they weren't committed and invested in the first place.

Ask yourself, Do I understand what this organization values, believes in, and hopes to be?

· · · · · · · · · · · · · · · · · ·

You can avoid these obstacles by creating a fresh and meaningful vision statement with the involvement of the entire faculty. The collective force and talent of the faculty is more likely to be realized when there is a common understanding of a shared vision. As Bamburg (1994) notes, "The schools that have been most successful in addressing and increasing the academic achievement of their students have benefited from a clarity of purpose that is grounded in a shared set of core values" (p. 14). We define *values* as the behaviors, beliefs, and actions that a school finds important.

The size of most schools' faculties prevents them from being as productive or as effective as smaller groups, but their full investment is still crucial. We recommend that you first form a team that, with training and guidance, will introduce the concept of a vision, facilitate and engage faculty in the process of writing one, and synthesize the multiple values and visions that the faculty develops. Ultimately, this team is the one putting together the pieces of the puzzle. This team may be made up of the members of the shared leadership team, or it could be composed of other staff members in the building as long as all departments are represented. Opting for the latter provides leadership opportunities for staff members who are not already formal teacher leaders. For our purposes here, we will refer to this collection of leaders as the vision oversight team.

Share Examples of Vision Statements

When you meet with the vision oversight team, sharing examples of vision statements with them is an important first step. This will help them better understand what a vision statement is, which in turn will help them assist the faculty when they facilitate its work. It's easy to find examples of real vision statements on the Internet. Here are a few to start with:

> Every Battlefield High School student will achieve personal success and become a responsible and productive citizen.
>
> —Battlefield High School,
> Prince William County Public Schools, Virginia

> The Richard Montgomery cluster will work collaboratively to ensure all students succeed. Placing the highest priority on reading and writing instruction will support consistent student achievement so that all students attain grade-level or higher performance levels annually, as measured by county, state, and national assessments. Partnerships across the cluster will sustain student success so that all students will read fluently by the end of Grade 2, write proficiently in both narrative and expository modes, pass algebra by the end of Grade 8, pass all High School Assessments on the first attempt, and graduate on schedule with the skills and knowledge required for success in higher education and/or the workplace.
>
> —Montgomery County Public Schools, Maryland

> Our vision, as a community, is to inspire a passion for learning.
>
> —John T. Baker Middle School,
> Montgomery County Public Schools, Maryland

> All Potomac Senior High School students will achieve personal success in their learning and become responsible and productive citizens.
>
> —Potomac Senior High School,
> Prince William County Public Schools, Virginia

> At Brentsville District we believe that all students can learn to their fullest potential. Student learning will be enhanced by national, global, and multicultural perspectives. Graduates will possess the basic knowledge and skills that will assure their proficiency in problem solving and technology. They will be

responsible citizens, lifelong learners, and will be prepared for a variety of postgraduation options.

—Brentsville District High School,
Prince William County Public Schools, Virginia

We will devote our human resources and technology to create superior products and services, thereby contributing to a better global society.

—Samsung Electronics, America

Our vision for the future is to be the customer's first and best choice in the products and services we provide.

—State Farm Insurance

There is a "Marriott Way." It's about serving the associates, the customer, and the community. Marriott's fundamental beliefs are enduring and the keys to its continued success.

—Marriott

After presenting these examples to the vision oversight team members, give them time to discuss their impressions of them with one another, and then lead a discussion with the entire team. You can ask the following questions to generate some dialogue on the statements:

- What patterns do you see in the statements?
- What do you like or dislike in the statements?
- Are the statements easy to understand?
- Are the statements too vague, or are they specific enough?
- Are they too long? Too short?
- Do the statements express an idea or a hope for the future?
- Are they too unambitious? Too "pie in the sky"?
- Do they contain adjectives or goals that are more appropriate for a mission statement?

• Do they clarify a direction for the school and for its improvement efforts?

You should also make sure to have copies of your school's current vision statement at the meeting so that participants can compare it with the examples. By discussing the current statement, the sample statements, the bulleted questions, and pertinent articles that you might wish to share as well, the vision oversight team should be able to reach an understanding of what makes a strong vision statement. You might also urge team members to explain to the faculty how the vision is a reflection of the school's values and hopes: it offers an opportunity to dream bigger, so stress to the team that it shouldn't let the faculty develop a "get-by statement," something that expresses a notion of mere adequacy. Tell team members to get the faculty to articulate what it is they truly want from their students and school. Graduation or job attainment is the bare minimum of what most educators hope for their students. The vision oversight team might consider having teachers brainstorm a list of adjectives or values and beliefs that will help them come up with an inspirational, compelling vision.

Present Data to the Vision Oversight Team

Before you involve the entire school in working toward a vision, you should first share some data with the vision oversight team. Doing so is important for two reasons. First, you want the vision oversight team to be familiar and comfortable with the data; since team members will in turn be sharing the data with the faculty, they should have a strong working knowledge of them so they are equipped to answer questions and help the staff understand what they are looking at. Second, as Bamburg (1994) observes, "Only when schools develop a shared understanding of current reality can a commitment to change be initiated and sustained" (p. 23). Reviewing data as an oversight team and then as a faculty is essential to help everyone identify where the school currently stands while also determining where they would like to be. Without a general understanding of the current data, the development of the vision could go in as many directions as there are opinions. The data provide a common, objective understanding and a solid foundation to build on.

Important data can be found everywhere in the daily, weekly, monthly, or yearly life of a school community. Too often, however, we associate data solely with student test results when there are other, sometimes more significant, data to examine. The vision oversight team and, eventually, the faculty should review

- Student attendance rates.
- Student tardies.
- Staff attendance rates and days most often missed.
- Department or grade-level staff absenteeism.
- Staff turnover rates.
- Student enrollment in sports or clubs.
- Disciplinary incidents (including types of referrals and where they occur among teachers, teams, and departments) and dispositions (including detention, in-school suspension, suspension, and expulsion).
- State assessment results.
- Local common assessment results.
- Standardized achievement test results.
- Advanced Placement (AP) test or International Baccalaureate (IB) test results.

Preloading the vision oversight team with these data will give team members the background knowledge they need to develop a vision in collaboration with the entire faculty.

Involve Staff in Developing the Vision

It is now time for the vision oversight team to involve the rest of the faculty in developing the vision statement. However they choose to present the examples of vision statements, data, and professional literature, be sure they give staff clear directions, specific questions, and definite time limits; the faculty will quickly discern fluff or a lack of organization, which will immediately turn them off. After they have had an opportunity to review and discuss the above items, they can craft their vision statement (see Resource 5).

First, the vision oversight team divides the staff into groups of no more than eight people. Then they ask each group to discuss the following questions:

Key ideas, values, and beliefs are the beginning of powerful visions.

- What evidence can you think of that we are meeting our current vision?
- What kind of school do we hope to be?
- What do you think should be reflected in our vision statement?
- What do we need to do differently to achieve this vision?
- How are we different from other schools?

Each group should have a scribe whose responsibility it is to record responses, ideas, and key terms and phrases that come up during group discussions. It is not necessary for groups to develop full sentences or statements at this point.

After group members have had a sufficient amount of time to share their thoughts with one another, each group should select someone to present the information to the rest of the staff. At this point, you also need to select a "master scribe" to maintain a master list of group responses on poster paper. The master scribe does not need to record duplications or similar phrases, although he or she may add checks or tally marks to indicate patterns or common ideas emerging from the faculty. The groups' presentations are an ideal time to validate responses, affirm staff members' commitment to education, and reinforce key ideas and values.

After each group has had the opportunity to share its information, the vision oversight team takes the master list and wordsmiths the key concepts and phrases into a vision statement—a one- or two-sentence statement that captures the faculty's image of the future. Some members of the team will be so excited by the good information they received from working with the faculty that they might find it hard to limit the vision to something so short. If so, you might have them work with the faculty to create a school "philosophy"—a lengthier paragraph that would extrapolate the vision. Next, each department receives a copy of the vision oversight team's draft vision to review, discuss, edit, and return to the team, which then makes appropriate adjustments to the statement.

When developing a vision, remember that less can be more; keep it short, and your staff will remember it longer.

The vision oversight team then unveils the vision statement to the entire staff at the next faculty meeting. At this point, you should celebrate your staff's considerable accomplishment in guiding school improvement efforts.

Drafting the Mission Statement

A mission statement is the wind that brings you to your desired harbor. It guides your travel and powers your momentum. Mission statements "give educators stronger motivation and provide parents with a clearer picture of what the school values. . . . A clear vision and a common mission that identify the kind of learning to be achieved can help keep the school and the efforts of its staff and students on target" (Peterson, 1995). Mission statements are the "how-to" statements or action plans that help schools achieve their vision. They prompt change and growth. The mission is the touch point that can help you determine whether what should be happening is, in fact, happening.

Share Examples of Mission Statements

The responsibility of crafting the mission statement can also lie with an oversight team or with the shared leadership team. Ideally, you would implement a process that echoes the vision development process by preloading the group with the information necessary to guide the staff in the development of a mission statement. Consider the following sample mission statements:

> At Battlefield Senior High School, we believe that student learning is the chief priority and all students can learn to their fullest potential. Students will develop their individual talents, critical thinking, and technology skills by being actively engaged in the learning process. Continuous commitment to improvement ensures that our students are well-rounded, self-directed, lifelong learners. By maintaining a safe and optimum learning environment, we provide the opportunity for students to be successful. Promoting high standards and expectations, teachers, administrators, parents, and the community share the responsibility for advancing the school's mission.
>
> —Battlefield High School,
> Prince William County Public Schools, Virginia

> In order to prepare students to live in and contribute to a changing world and engage in active, lifelong learning, Richard Montgomery High School provides a balanced, varied school curriculum designed to meet the academic, cultural, and social needs of individuals from the diverse backgrounds of our community.
>
> —Richard Montgomery High School,
> Montgomery County Public Schools, Maryland

> John T. Baker Middle School seeks to be an exemplary learning community school. We build the foundation of this community through meaningful relationships, relevant and engaging learning, and effective communication. We challenge ourselves to be better than we think we can be, and advocate for the greater good of our multidimensional community. Our success in this mission will build lifelong, confident learners, who have the tools necessary for success in a changing world.
>
> —John T. Baker Middle School,
> Montgomery County Public Schools, Maryland

> Our mission is to empower all students to apply their acquired skills and knowledge, and to rely upon their personal attributes to lead productive lives and to become contributing members of the global community.
>
> —Potomac Senior High School,
> Prince William County Public Schools, Virginia

Our mission is to provide a high-quality, comprehensive, and meaningful education for all students. Each student will be expected to succeed within the bounds of their abilities and chosen educational goals. Each student will be treated as an individual, given the tools to be a lifelong learner, and taught to function as a member of a group and as a productive member of society.

—Brentsville District High School,
Prince William County Public Schools, Virginia

State Farm's mission is to help people manage the risks of everyday life, recover from the unexpected and realize their dreams.

—State Farm Insurance

FedEx will produce superior financial returns for shareowners by providing high value-added supply chain, transportation, business and related information services through focused operating companies. Customer requirements will be met in the highest quality manner appropriate to each market segment served. FedEx will strive to develop mutually rewarding relationships with its employees, partners and suppliers. Safety will be the first consideration in all operations. Corporate activities will be conducted to the highest ethical and professional standards.

—FedEx

To continually provide our members with quality goods and services at the lowest possible prices.

—Costco Wholesale

This range of examples should spark some discussion among mission oversight team members. You can ask the following questions to generate dialogue on the statements:

• What patterns do you see in the statements?

• Are the statements specific enough?

• Do the statements simply state a belief, or do they express a purpose for existence?

- Do the statements clarify what action steps students and staff will be expected to take to achieve the vision?
- Do the statements clarify how staff will engage in improvement efforts?

The mission statement should encompass the values of the staff, the actions that the school will take, and the areas it will address (e.g., curriculum, assessments, data) to achieve its vision. The mission statement should be longer than the vision statement because it is a specific plan for driving the school to fulfill its potential (see Resource 6).

After the faculty has worked on the mission using the same procedures they used in developing the vision, the mission oversight team again attempts to blend key words, phrases, and concepts into a viable statement. During this process, they need to ensure that the mission they are crafting aligns with the new vision statement—specifically, that the steps, actions, and values stated in the mission are things that will help them achieve the vision. The relationship between the mission and the vision must be clear.

After the mission oversight team has completed the draft, it is sent back to the faculty for review and discussion. Then the team meets again to review the feedback and make necessary adjustments before a final unveiling to the staff.

After the school has adopted the final drafts of both the mission and the vision, invite multimedia or art classes to design posters prominently displaying the statements. Soliciting these classes' assistance saves money and is a good way to make the vision and mission a meaningful part

Repetition, design, and placement are strategic ways to keep the mission alive.

of students' lives. The vision and mission should be sent home in newsletters and posted in prominent gathering places throughout the school—classrooms, the mailroom, the lunchroom, and so on—to keep it at the forefront of people's minds.

Define What You Intend to Accomplish

The school's next step is to devise a plan to fulfill its mission. The SMART format—a widely used method for developing goals in schools and businesses—provides a framework for developing goals and action steps to help you focus on what really needs to be done. *SMART* stands for *S*pecific, *M*easurable, *A*chievable, *R*elevant, and *T*ime Frame. Figure 2.1 demonstrates the difference between traditional goals and progressive SMART goals. You can use this table as a guideline to develop your goals, checking to make sure that they meet the five parameters.

After creating your goals, the next step is to develop SMART action steps—tasks or activities that you will engage in to achieve the goals. Figure 2.2 depicts an action step developed to help meet the SMART goal in Figure 2.1.

Specificity and clarity are key elements. When developing each goal and action step, consider the following questions:

- **Why** does it need to be done?
- **Who** will be affected, who is responsible, and who will participate? Who is the audience, and who are the stakeholders?
- **What** needs to be done? The "what" should be in direct relation to the purpose.
- **When** will this take place? When will we know we are done? When can our progress be measured?
- **How** will it be measured? How will you know it was successful?

Using Vision and Mission to Focus School Improvement

The school improvement plan (SIP) is the tool that will help you get the most out of your vision, mission, and goals. It is a more detailed document than the mission and vision statements. Like the mission statement, it falls within the scope of the vision.

Figure 2.1	Analysis of a Traditional Goal and a Progressive Goal Using the SMART Framework	
	Traditional Goal	**Progressive Goal**
	Student achievement will improve.	The passing rate of limited-English-proficient students will increase from 79 percent to 85 percent on the Algebra I Standards of Learning (SOL) exam in 2008.
Specific	This goal needs more specificity. Which students from our population will improve? What aspect of their achievement do we want to see improved? Marking period grades? Final course grades? Standardized test scores? The desired outcome is unclear.	This goal identifies a subgroup, a subject, and a target population and clearly defines the desired outcome. We could even break this down further by identifying a tested strand on this SOL.
Measurable	"Improve" is difficult to quantify. What does it really mean? By how much do we want achievement to improve?	This goal is measurable. It clearly identifies the starting point as 79 percent and the minimal acceptable value as 85 percent.
Achievable	This goal *seems* achievable. But we do not really know because the goal does not define what it means by "improve."	You can gauge whether a goal is achievable by asking yourself if the goal is pushing you beyond your limits or if it is something you can accomplish if you stretch yourself. A goal of improving to a 100 percent passing rate in one year would not be reasonable, but a 6 percent increase is.
Relevant	Is this goal relevant to the school's vision and mission? We can't tell because the goal is not clear on how it relates to them.	This goal is relevant because it has identified a specific area of need. It is standards-based and directly addresses academic achievement.
Time Frame	What is the time frame for reaching this goal? We have no idea whether it's a short-term goal or a long-range goal.	The end date for this goal is the 2008 main testing window.

Figure 2.2	Development of an Action Step Using the SMART Framework
	Action Step
	Teachers will incorporate foldables and graphic organizers into their Algebra I class to reinforce new terminology.
Specific	The action step names two specific strategies and clearly states expectations.
Measurable	Teachers can measure their application of the strategies against lesson plans or team minutes.
Achievable	The strategies are achievable because teachers on the Algebra I team who know how to use foldables and graphic organizers agreed to share their expertise with the rest of the team.
Relevant	This is a relevant action step because achievement has been low and limited-English-proficient students have expressed difficulty learning the vocabulary in Algebra I.
Time Frame	These strategies will be incorporated when new terminology is introduced in the class.

The SIP is a blueprint for the school's progress toward its goals. It helps propel grade-level teams, curriculum teams, and departments toward meaningful improvement. It provides detailed expectations for administrators, teachers, counselors, and other stakeholders and includes specific plans that guide improvement efforts throughout the year. Although the majority of school improvement plans focus on improving student achievement through such measures as high-stakes tests, advanced placement exams, and the SAT, we recommend enriching the document to include several areas outside the realm of assessment. For example, you might add a section about improving student attendance or reducing the number of disciplinary infractions. You could seek to increase participation in extracurricular activities and athletics and improve the delivery of student services offered by the guidance department, the career center, and the library. Use your SIP as an opportunity to develop goals, plans, and actions to improve all facets of your school's life.

Keep in mind the following points as you develop your school improvement plan:

> *If we ask students to create a plan for their improvement, we should be open to doing the same for ourselves.*

- Make sure the plan includes a proposal for staff development. If teachers aren't learning and growing, it is not likely that students are either.

- An improvement plan is only useful when it is doable. All goals that are developed by each department in the school should fall under the umbrella of the school system's goals and objectives; if not, you could be trying to do too much or go in too many directions and will end up accomplishing very little.

- The SIP should help you not only look forward but also evaluate what has been done in the past. Without such reflection, your efforts will be random, unfocused, and unsupported.

Building the School Improvement Plan

A high-quality school improvement plan is essential for establishing and maintaining a healthy culture. Because of its importance, the shaping of and responsibility for the SIP must not rest in the hands of a select few. In successful schools we have worked in, a group of representative staff members referred to as the SIP team is assigned to work with school staff to identify areas of need and develop action plans, which are the specific steps and tasks articulated to achieve the stated goals. The SIP team typically consists of department chairs, team leaders, administrators, a parent representative, and at least one support staff member, such as a secretary or an instructional assistant. However, we recommend involving potential teacher leaders in the development of the SIP as well. You should conduct the selection process for the SIP team each year to allow everyone the opportunity to participate. In some schools where we have worked, these positions were highly sought after because they offered opportunities for professional growth.

We recommend that the team include stakeholders who will be affected by the content of the SIP. At the very least, the team should include a representative from each department, whether it's the department chair or another staff member (although we do not suggest recruiting a novice teacher). The representative does not hold sole responsibility for developing his or her department's portion of the SIP; rather, he or she facilitates the collection of the information that the department will include. The representative is expected to conduct meetings with department members to discuss what should be included in the SIP, establish deadlines for submitting this information, polish the information, and return it to his or her departmental colleagues for final approval before submitting it for inclusion in the school's master SIP document.

Formatting the School Improvement Plan

The best way to identify the essential details for your school's SIP is to consult school staff during the SIP development process. If your school does not already have a prescribed format, you can use the following list as a starting point. These are all items that will add value to your SIP. Note that we are not suggesting you include everything in the list below in your SIP, nor do we claim that the list is a complete list of everything your school or school system needs to consider when developing its improvement plan:

1. *Cover page*. This should include the title, your school's name, and the date.

2. *Committee member list*. This should include the name and title of each member of the SIP team.

3. *State department vision and mission statements*. Most state departments of education have a published vision and mission.

4. *School system vision and mission statements*. Most school systems have a published vision and mission.

5. *The school's vision and mission statements.* The overarching components of the school's vision and mission should fall within the parameters of the school system's vision and mission. If the school system does not have vision and mission statements, we still recommend that your school develop its own.

6. *School details and demographics.* This includes school statistics on ethnicity; gender; English proficiency; economic status; educational designation (e.g., general education, gifted, special education, and twice exceptional); graduation rates; percentage of last year's students who enrolled in a two-year or four-year college or trade school; and enrollment in AP/IB courses.

7. *NCLB AYP Report Card or High-Stakes Report (depending on the state).* If provided by the state, include a report of the most recent AYP results for your school by subject, grade, and subgroup status.

8. *School system goals and objectives (if available).* These are typically created by the school board and/or the superintendent's office. They may be referred to as objectives or targets, among other descriptors.

9. *SIP calendar.* The calendar should include the dates and times when the SIP team is expected to meet and when it is expected to deliver content and evidence of efforts and completion.

10. *Departmental goals.* These goals focus on improving student achievement or delivery of services (for example, from the guidance department, the main office, and so on) specific to each department or team.

11. *Indicators of achievement.* These are specific indicators or results that will be reviewed to determine effectiveness.

12. *Areas of focus.* These include specific content areas, skills, standards, anchors, populations, and services that are targeted in the SIP.

13. *Action plans for each department or grade-level team.* Each department's specific action plan includes data sources, point of

contact, potential costs, staff development efforts, required materials, activities, and time line to put the action plan in place and measure its effect.

The sections of the school improvement plan that are specific to individual departments and grade-level teams should provide focus for each of the areas with regard to content delivery. For example, in our version, items 10–13 would include any department in the building. In this case, we use the math department as an example, which might have an overall goal such as "Student passing rates on the Geometry Standards of Learning [Virginia's year-end high-stakes assessment] will improve from 81 percent to 86 percent in the following year." In some cases, the goal may target certain populations, such as "The percentage of African American students successfully completing geometry will increase from 73 percent to 80 percent by the end of the following school year." Departments and grade-level teams should measure their efforts and indicators of effectiveness against these goals on a monthly basis to obtain objective information to fuel their discussions.

We purposely mention "areas of focus" in item 12 to hone efforts and add value to departmental discussions about curriculum delivery. In this section of the SIP you would find statements such as "During the 2008–2009 school year, the mathematics department will increase focus on (1) patterns, functions, and algebra and (2) numbers and number sense." At least once a month, the department or team should assess the extent to which its content delivery hit these specific areas of focus.

Reviewing the School Improvement Plan

When the SIP is finalized, it should become a public document, accessible to all staff. Posting the SIP electronically will save paper and photocopying expenses, although you might want to divide the document by department or team and print a hard copy of each section.

We encourage schools to conduct quarterly reviews of the SIP and periodically monitor their progress. Item 13 of the SIP includes timelines for completion and evidence of attainment. These checkpoints are a good time to assess the extent to which teams are following through on their action plans. Waiting until the end of the year to conduct reviews will prevent staff from making needed changes along the way, and the following year may start with a stagnant, less-than-effective SIP.

Realizing Your Vision and Mission

Vision and mission statements provide schools with an essential overview of where they want to go and what they want to be. Few thriving schools or companies attained their success without developing such statements as elements of their school improvement plans or business plans. But merely drafting statements is not enough. To realize your school's vision and mission, you must model your school's beliefs, values, and collective commitments while demonstrating enthusiasm for what will come next. Perhaps most important, your vision and mission establish clear expectations and standards for your staff. We further discuss how to get the most out of your staff in the following chapter.

Getting Started

- Identify and train vision and mission oversight teams.
- If there are existing vision and mission statements, review them to determine their relevance and accuracy.
- Devise a meaningful plan to involve the staff in either revising the existing vision and mission statements or creating new ones.
- Ask probing questions to guide staff in developing their vision and mission.

3

Promoting Excellence Among Your Staff

We have all worked with at least one teacher who should have retired years ago, or who should never have entered the profession. Some lucky students—generally those who are self-sufficient and motivated and who have a strong outside support structure—learn in spite of these teachers. But what happens to those who don't even have the bare bones of proficiency? Or those who need some inspiration to unleash their potential? All students, regardless of their talent or motivation, need someone to coach them and stretch their abilities.

Providing this level of support to students can be intimidating even for talented and veteran teachers, and it is downright overwhelming to those who are not as well equipped to meet the challenge. One of your roles as a leader is to help your teachers grow as professionals. You need to build on their strengths, tap into their talents, and promote the belief that everyone can learn from one another.

Value Your Staff

Before you embark on any major change effort, assure teachers that you need their talent, candor, and input to work and succeed as a team. Clearly communicating that you expect them to act as contributing members of the team shows that you recognize their expertise and increases morale. Teachers who feel valued are generally more productive and have a greater interest and investment in their school.

Demonstrating trust and respect will in turn earn trust and respect.

If teachers sense that you do not value them, on the other hand, you can bank on resistance to change. You will have difficulty building leadership, trust, and respect. Unappreciated or unsupported, staff members may transfer to another school to find a more supportive and nurturing environment, or they may lose their motivation and begin to just collect paychecks. Seeing the school's main entrance as a revolving door takes a significant toll on morale. Staff turnover also takes a financial toll: according to the U.S. Department of Labor, the turnover of one teacher costs a district slightly more than $12,000 (Alliance for Excellent Education, 2005). For all these reasons, it is in your best interest to invest in ways to retain your teachers and demonstrate that you value them.

Acknowledge Experience

How many times have you heard a teacher say, "I've been teaching for 20 years," followed by a justification for why he or she is right, or why something else is wrong? Educators want to be recognized for the time they have dedicated to helping other people's children. You can provide this recognition. The first day of summer inservice or the first faculty meeting of the year is a good time to do so.

Have teachers form a line ranking themselves according to years of experience, from least to most. Then ask teachers to introduce themselves one by one and reveal the number of years they have been in education. Have one person keep track of the years of experience and then tally the total at the end of the introductions. Teachers are usually astonished when they hear the collective number of years of educational experience in the room. Recognize and applaud this total! Then point out that the total number of years of educational experience far surpasses any individual teacher's experience, and strongly advise teachers to tap into the expertise surrounding them. Encourage collegiality by reminding staff that no one is able to benefit from all this knowledge and experience by working in isolation.

Share the Smiles

One middle school principal we worked with kept a running agenda item at faculty meetings called "Smiles," a time when he would share an anecdote about something he had observed since the last meeting that made him smile. For example, a few days before one meeting he caught a student running in the halls between classes. When he stopped the student, she apologized for breaking the rules but explained that she didn't want to be late for her teacher's class because she was so excited about the activity for that day. The learning environment that the teacher had created caused a student to want to be in class so much that she was willing to break the rules in front of the principal! Even as he reminded the girl of the rules, he could not help but smile at all the good things that were happening in the building. At the faculty meeting, he relayed this anecdote, referring to the girl's teacher by name. Then he asked teachers to share their own "smiles" with their colleagues.

There is a lot to smile about in your building or on your team; bring the smiles to the surface to share with others.

When you try this in your meetings, keep in mind that some staff members will be reluctant to share at first. They may be uncomfortable in the spotlight or may not want to seem too eager to go along with something new, for example. Be prepared to call on a reliable staff member, possibly someone you have spoken with in advance, to share. You might get the practice started by saying, "Mrs. James, could you share with us that fascinating lab your class did last week?" When she is done, encourage her to call on someone else to share next.

This kind of recognition is a simple way of showing teachers that you are paying attention to their efforts and expertise. It also clarifies expectations and reinforces the values of the school.

Give Time

Many teachers need just one thing to feel valued: your time. Yes, time is scarce. But the leader who spares the time to hear about a teacher's problem with a class or about an event in his or her personal life will find that this investment yields high dividends.

An open-door policy that invites colleagues to come in and talk whenever they need to is a great start, but the office environment does not readily lend itself to sacrosanct time for conversations. As welcoming as you might be, the "ping" signaling a new e-mail or the ring of a transferred phone call can be distracting. To remedy this, several principals we know hold events like "Coffee with the Principal," during which they remain in a teacher workroom all day, ignoring nonemergency calls and e-mails to talk with colleagues over coffee.

Staff members in these schools appreciate this face time and look forward to chatting with their principals. In turn, the principals are able to learn more about their teachers' lives and find out what teachers truly think about certain issues. Staff members tend to be more comfortable sharing their thoughts and concerns in such a relaxed, informal environment.

Because time is so scarce, teachers appreciate it more than anything else their leaders give them.

Another way to make yourself accessible in an unofficial capacity is to bring your lunch to school. Administrators often miss lunch due to multiple pressing demands, or they eat on the fly, in the cafeteria while on duty, or in isolation while they address their responsibilities. Occasionally bringing in a brown-bag lunch and choosing to spend the small amount of free time you have eating with your teachers shows that you value them. Keep in mind that you also need to respect *their* free time by not engaging in professional conversation unless they initiate it.

Implement Peer Observations

Some teachers embrace the idea of peer observation, while others prefer isolation. A question we ask both kinds of teachers to illustrate the benefits of peer observation is, Where did you learn your best lesson or get your best idea? (See Resource 7.) Almost invariably, the response is that

The best teachers are the best thieves, as the saying goes.

it came from another teacher—not a college course, textbook, or video. Many teachers identify their teaching practicum as a particularly fruitful period. During this training and preparation time, we all learned from a higher level of expertise and were able to observe and exchange dialogue with a broad range of teachers about best practices. When we discuss strategies and ideas with colleagues, we often discover that these esteemed mentors picked up many of their own practices from other teachers.

Simply put, we learn best from others, and we are better teachers because of others. Yet many schools don't have a system of peer observations—and many teachers feel threatened at the prospect of them. Therefore, when you first implement this practice, involve your teachers in the process, and be prepared for the following questions:

- When do we enter the room—before the bell has rung or during instruction?
- How long do we have to stay in the class?
- How do we communicate our feedback?

- By when do we have to give feedback?
- How many observations must we do?
- What is the purpose of the observation?
- What do we do if we don't see anything positive to comment on?

Most of these are instructional questions and, as such, should be addressed by the shared leadership team and the faculty in general. We recommend that the administrator or teacher leader facilitate a discussion and let the instructional specialists answer most of these questions.

Administrators, remember to model the desired behaviors. Peer observations are good for you, too.

The exceptions are the last two questions. In these cases, you might be better equipped to guide the conversation. Of course, you wouldn't open the discussion by saying, "Here is what you do when you observe a terrible teacher," but you can list some of the elements in the list below as "look-for's" during observations. Sharing them also serves as a good reinforcement of your expectations, a reminder of some of the finer points of classroom instruction, and a resource for teachers if they are stumped for something to comment on.

- Classroom environment.
- Room arrangement.
- Student work displays.
- Teacher-made displays.
- Teacher mobility.
- Wait time I and II.
- Percentage of students participating.
- Percentage of minority students participating.
- Percentages of male and female students called on.

- Management of attendance procedures.
- Collection and distribution of work.
- Handling of interruptions (e.g., PA announcements, visitors at the door, fire drills).
- Positive interactions.
- Praise and respect.
- Support of school rules.
- Use of technology.

Although not all of these elements are directly tied to instructional technique, most are linked to content delivery and have a significant effect on the learning environment, so they are worth highlighting if observed.

The shared leadership team should develop a form for teachers to fill out during peer observations. This form is another way to develop capacity on the leadership team; team members can discuss "look-for's" in the classroom, devise the observation tool, and bring it back to their respective departments for feedback. The form need not be an elaborate one, though (see Resource 8). Consider creating it on NCR paper to make it easier to provide a copy to the teacher being observed, the department chair or team leader, and the assistant principal.

Some teachers express concern over administrators receiving a copy of the form. In most instances, they fear that the peer observation will be used in their evaluation. You should not formally factor these forms into teacher evaluations, but they do reveal which practices teachers are using and which teachers might be able to provide support and modeling for struggling teachers. In some cases, the information will bring concerns to light (or confirm existing concerns), signaling you to begin making formal observations.

Ensure Observations

By the end of the first marking period, you should touch base with teachers who have not yet conducted a peer observation. Don't open the discussion by addressing their noncompliance; rather, talk to them about observation as an opportunity for professional growth, and let them know that you value what they have to offer their colleagues. You should have these discussions early in the school year. Just as teachers do for long-term assignments, provide short-term checkpoints before the final product is due.

If after the initial conference staff members still haven't participated, it is time to begin documenting the insubordination (see Resource 9). There will probably be teachers who still haven't conducted a peer observation by the third marking period. By that point, your conferences, documentation, and intuition should give you a handle on whether this is procrastination or insubordination. In either case, at this late stage you should give the teachers a drop-dead date. After that date has passed, treat those who haven't conducted an observation as insubordinate.

In general, administrators should be highly involved in the peer observation process. Without your strong involvement and commitment, only a handful of teachers will participate, and the initiative will likely fade away. We suggest introducing a peer observation apparatus during a summer inservice day or at the first faculty meeting. If your school holds a welcome-back breakfast or lunch, introduce the initiative then to associate it with something positive.

To begin, give the teachers a blank index card for each class period they teach and have them fill out a card for each class, including the course title and their names. Set up a table with several boxes—one for each class period of the day—and have the teachers drop their cards into the appropriate boxes. Then have each teacher draw a card from a box that represents a period when he or she is not in class. The name that is drawn is the colleague whom the teacher will observe. This process is not a perfect model, especially since schools have different structures and schedules in place, so you may have to do some juggling to ensure that everyone has a person to observe. However, this method helps you sidestep any accusations that you are purposely assigning specific teachers to observe certain other teachers.

The process we have described allows for only one peer observation during the school year. Once peer observation becomes an accepted part of your school's culture, however, you can duplicate the process midyear or even quarterly.

Identify Best Practices

Peer observations enable teachers to network more with their colleagues, develop a better understanding of different grade levels and subjects, and identify best practices. However, if you truly want to get the most out of your teachers and disseminate best practices—not simply satisfy someone else's mandate—you need to take the observations to the next level. Engage your teacher leaders in discussions about the specific best practices, good ideas, and "aha!" moments that their teachers have observed that everyone should know about. Examine and discuss "look-for's" in the following areas:

- **Environment.** For this area, look for practices that enable the smooth operation of the classroom. The teacher engages students quickly at the beginning of the lesson with a warm-up that he or she has posted before they enter the room. A daily agenda remains on the board for the entire period, and the teacher consistently posts homework assignments in the same place. The teacher completes administrative tasks, such as attendance, in an unobtrusive manner. Transitions flow seamlessly, and students and teacher have a respectful rapport.

- **Instruction.** The teacher differentiates instruction and uses a variety of instructional techniques to meet different learning modalities (tactile, kinesthetic, visual, and so on). The teacher encourages struggling students and challenges the more advanced students. The teacher provides opportunities for guided and independent practice and breaks the class period into smaller learning periods to keep students on task. At the end of class, the teacher summarizes key concepts and skills and previews the next lesson. In a team-taught setting, an important "look-for" is a balance in teaching responsibilities. Besides assessing the teachers' collaboration in delivering the content and managing the class, the observer is ideally not able to differentiate the primary teacher from the team teacher.

• **Expectations.** The teacher clearly communicates behavioral and learning expectations, and students behave appropriately with little guidance or redirection. The teacher addresses off-task behavior in a nonconfrontational manner, through proximity, humor, or reminder of expectations. The teacher delivers instruction and directions logically and communicates high expectations for students.

• **Technology.** Teachers and students use technology to enhance learning, including such tools as computers, presentation software, personal response systems, videos, podcasts, the Internet, interactive whiteboards, and global positioning systems. Students are required to use technology when making presentations and demonstrations.

• **Instructional questioning.** The teacher bases his or her questions on the cognitive domains of the revised Bloom's Taxonomy: remember, understand, apply, analyze, evaluate, and create (Anderson & Krathwohl, 2001). The teacher provides appropriate wait time for each question, calls on students by name, and asks students to discuss the response. The teacher redirects the question when necessary and encourages students to develop their own questions.

• **Communication.** This element applies mostly to team-taught settings. Students ask either teacher for support or clarification about an assignment or their grades. Both teachers take responsibility in assigning homework, introducing new assignments or activities, and responding to behavior issues.

Model the process of identifying and discussing these observed strategies and ideas to your teacher leaders, then ask them to repeat the process with their own teams or departments. Departments could even target certain "look-for's" in their observations. For example, for one marking period, a department might choose to focus on classroom environment, then share and discuss strategies

A best practice is not simply what a teacher likes to do or is good at; it must also be something that produces desired results.

and ideas that teachers observed in that area. Then the teacher leaders can bring those identified practices back to the leadership team for sharing and discussion; the ultimate goal is to present and model the best practices at faculty meetings or other events that reach the entire staff.

You could also have teachers fill out best practices worksheets during a faculty meeting or an inservice (see Resource 10). Provide a few minutes for them to think about one or two of their own effective teaching practices, then divide the staff into groups of five, making sure to group teachers who don't work together on a daily basis. Allot each group member three minutes—one minute to share their best practices while the others take notes, and two minutes to answer clarifying questions from the other group members. During this activity, teachers should keep an open mind to others' strategies and refrain from challenging any practices shared.

After everyone has had an opportunity to share his or her best practices, have staff members form new groups by department or grade level. Have these new groups repeat the sharing process, allowing for a cross-migration of best practices throughout the school. To expand the application of these practices, each department or team could try adopting a strategy for a week or a month and then switch to another. You could charge each team with finding one practice that team members think could work in every classroom and bringing their suggestion to the next inservice or faculty meeting for consideration.

Not only teachers should conduct peer observations; leadership team members and building administrators should participate as well. Leadership team members can observe fellow team members facilitating department or grade-level team meetings, for example. Although leaders sometimes hesitate to see how other administrators conduct business, if it is good for teachers, how could it not be good for them as well?

Homegrown Professional Development

Most schools' faculty meetings are purely informational. Their only educational aspect, if they have one, is generally training in some new kind of tool—a software application or the mobile computer lab reservation process, for example. These kinds of demonstrations are what usually pass as in-house staff development.

A better use of time would be to model ways for teachers to integrate these learning applications into their delivery of content and to demonstrate the effect they will have on instruction and learning. To illustrate, imagine that two different schools are introducing a personal response system at their respective faculty meetings. In one school, the technology coordinator hooks up the system and explains the setup—how the clickers work, how the monitor displays the results, and how teachers can sign out the equipment. In the other school, after a similar explanation of the technology, the staff uses the system to respond to a few survey questions administered by the shared leadership team to evaluate the effectiveness of a specific initiative. The system then displays the survey results for the entire room to see, and staff members discuss how they might use this technology in their own classrooms, sharing specific ideas and examples. Which of these two sets of teachers do you think is more likely to use the new technology?

Although you can devise a lesson for a faculty meeting easily enough, delivering information meaningfully is an intensive process. For example, at a middle school where we were charged with explaining AYP Safe Harbor status, we could have just handed out a memo. Instead, we decided to teach the staff the meaning of Safe Harbor and what the school would need to accomplish in the following year to meet AYP standards and qualify for the Safe Harbor provision.

First, we shared state AYP requirements with the staff through an overhead presentation and handouts. Next, we compared the school's results from the previous year's high-stakes tests with AYP requirements. We then presented the formula for calculating a school's eligibility for Safe Harbor and asked each attendee to apply the formula to last year's results to identify the minimum amount of growth required to be eligible for Safe Harbor for the current year. Participants shared their findings with their neighbors, and then we reviewed the correct answers as a group and discussed the findings using the Think-Pair-Share strategy. By the end of the meeting, all staff members were able to articulate the meaning of AYP Safe Harbor and knew exactly how much they needed to improve in the previous year's deficient areas.

Facilitate Professional Collaboration

It's relatively easy to make scheduling adjustments to allow teachers time for planning and collaboration. The hard part—knowing how to use that time—is up to teachers. Teachers are often unable to articulate what their collaboration should look like because they are not used to working so collegially. As an exercise, try asking each member of a grade-level team or department to write down a brief interpretation of collaboration on their team, then have the teachers share their opinions with one another.

If your staff members are like most, they will have varying ideas on what collaboration means. For some, it is a time to talk about what they are teaching; for others, it is an opportunity to discuss students. Still others see it is a chance to complain about colleagues, parents, and supervisors. And all too often, it becomes a time to talk about the finer points of weddings, child rearing, and car mechanics. Thus, you will need to clarify your expectations for what should happen during allotted collaboration time.

Use the Best to Guide the Rest

As a leader, you need to make it clear to teachers that their collaboration efforts should specifically focus on school improvement. You can start by opening a dialogue on how teachers identify essential learning expectations and communicate them to staff, students, and parents. Then discuss ways in which their classroom practices contribute to the goals of the school and school district. For example, discuss instructional strategies that could be implemented in classrooms by department, grade, or curriculum team to enhance learning.

Analyzing curriculum is another great starting point for teacher collaboration. Although many school systems provide scope and sequence guides, the teachers who are actually supposed to use them often find them irrelevant or unrealistic for their students and thus seldom adhere to them closely. It would be far more useful to guide your teachers in auditing the scope and sequence of the curriculum to determine its appropriateness and assess the pacing.

Make sure your best teachers help other teachers grow. The better they are, the more the system needs them.

Planning lessons and units of study is another ideal way for teachers to collaborate. You might initiate collaboration by asking teams to consider and discuss the questions below:

- What are the "big ticket" items for this unit? What should every student know and be able to do by the end of the unit, marking period, or semester?

- What are the essential questions that will guide our focus and enhance student interest and inquiry?

- Are there other topics we might want to cover along the way to our destination? Are there areas that will complement the key ideas and issues of the unit?
- How will we know whether we have achieved our objectives?
- How will we assess student learning and measure their success?
- What materials could we use to get students to that point?
- How much time do we estimate we'll need to cover this area of study? (Gabriel, 2005, p. 130)

To begin answering these questions, teachers can fill in blank calendars with the skills or concepts to be taught and the number of days they think they will need to cover them. A benefit to collaborative lesson planning is that it gives teachers a built-in support system to help them in the delivery of content. Some veteran teachers may try to get out of planning as a team by claiming that they don't need a support system. Tell them that if they are that talented, they will be a valuable asset to the less experienced teachers and are thus an indispensable part of the support system.

You also need to ensure that teachers agree on checkpoints for administering common assessments so that the team can maintain pacing, check for learning, analyze data, and adjust curriculum as needed. Their discussions should center on how students in each teacher's class are faring on particular skills and concepts and whether adjustments are necessary; they can examine student work for patterns in mistakes and errors. Teachers could also decide whether they need to spend more time on a particular skill or concept.

Some teachers will have a bigger learning curve than others in terms of functioning as part of a team. Meetings may resemble free-for-alls, with team members talking over one another and no clear purpose or expectations. This kind of scenario is more common than you might think. In Chapter 6, we discuss in further depth ways to help your teachers collaborate better.

Develop Your Own Formative Assessments

It is essential to provide opportunities for teachers to create, implement, and analyze the results of formative assessments. As Marzano (2006) writes, "Research supports the conclusion that formative classroom assessment is one of the most powerful tools a classroom teacher might use."

Some students confuse formative assessments with summative assessments. You should explain that unlike summative assessments, which measure learning at the end of a unit or course and inform the final grade, formative assessments are designed as a sort of ongoing status check to assess students' learning and inform teachers' instruction. One way to offer clarification is to compare a formative assessment to a speedometer: just as a speedometer informs the driver whether the car is moving below, at, or above the posted speed limit, formative assessment data communicate to students their academic pace. Just as the driver uses the information received from the speedometer to make decisions about adjusting his or her speed, students can use formative assessment data to adjust their own learning.

It is also important to make sure that the faculty reaches a collective understanding on the nature and purpose of formative assessments. We have worked with teachers who challenged the formative/summative divide and argued that the assessments do not have to be one or the other, that they can serve more than one function. Therefore, all staff members need to calibrate their definitions of the assessment types before they can move ahead in collaboratively developing and administering formative assessments.

The next step for many school leaders is to help teachers identify what they want to improve through formative assessments. Often, the targeted area is state assessment results. After some discussion, staff members will generally agree that they need to align their formative assessments with the state's assessment blueprint and framework. Many state departments of education post this information on their Web sites. In schools where we have worked, staff actively researched the state test structure and format and used them as a model for their formative assessments throughout the year. They looked at such details as question format, the weight given to different skills, the difficulty level of the reading passages, and the order of distracters. As teachers got better at aligning their own assessments with the state's assessments, students demonstrated increased proficiency on that type of assessment. (One caveat: Obviously, state assessments are not the only, or the best, vehicle to measure proficiency. They are best used in conjunction with alternative forms of assessment, such as projects, presentations, and portfolios.)

As a leader, you will need to provide some guidance as the teams devise their assessments. This support can take the form of in-house training and professional literature reviews, but it is most helpful to actively enlist your teachers in the effort of identifying a process to follow or adapt. After discussing formative assessments and their benefits with the shared leadership team and developing an understanding among all staff members on the nature and purpose of the assessments, the faculty can begin the collaborative process of developing common formative assessments using the following guidelines:

- Reach consensus on the format of the assessment, the skills it will cover, the time allotted to students to complete the assessment, the frequency of assessments, and the time windows for administering the assessments.

- Identify a minimum and maximum number of items (questions) for each assessment.

- Align the format and design of the test with those of the state assessment.

- Make sure each item relates to a specific skill outlined in the curriculum.

- Include one correct answer and three plausible distracters for each multiple-choice item.
- Establish guidelines for the length of the assessment.
- Ensure that assessments are in manageable "chunks" rather than "jumbo" tests.
- Agree to bring one or more assessment items to the next collaboration session.
- Combine the items everyone brought and draft the first copy of the assessment.
- Review the assessment to certify that it meets the agreed-upon guidelines.
- Supply the department chair and the administrator with a copy of the assessment and a specific date for completion.

When initiating the use of common formative assessments, be sure to recognize your staff's current expertise in assessing student learning.

Following these procedures and creating a common format make it easy to interpret results for each assessment item. The information enables both students and teachers to make decisions based on the students' strengths and areas of need. Once students receive the assessment results, they can develop a plan of action with the teacher to improve specific skills. This is a far more effective approach for reaching desired goals than just providing students with a raw score on a summative test in a specific subject, which may lead students to decide that they're either good or not good at the subject and might as well not bother trying to improve, especially since the unit has just ended.

Engage Your Staff in Book Studies and Professional Development

A simple way to foster professional development is to place copies of current articles on educational practice in teachers' mailboxes or e-mail the articles out. In one school we worked in, this strategy grew over time, and teachers started occasionally distributing articles themselves. Not everyone read all the articles, but those who were aggressively pursuing their careers or who wanted to improve their practice did.

At this school, these articles became watercooler talk. Those who read the articles wanted to discuss the content, which piqued the interest of those who hadn't read the articles but didn't want to be left out of the loop. Gradually, the school became a faculty of readers.

This type of professional development can be executed by the administration and modeled by team leaders and department chairs. Teachers can read the literature distributed by the building's leadership, or the team leader can disseminate content-specific reading. Either way, the team should actively question and discuss the issues at hand. Teachers can even read and discuss shorter articles during meetings; longer pieces can be broken down and assigned to team members who can later report on what they have read and how the central ideas relate to their classroom.

Team members should experiment with strategies and ideas they read about and then share their success or failure with the group. They can also present minilessons and activities to their colleagues. If there is a professional library in the school or at the central office, members can borrow professional videos to view and discuss. If there are no such resources, teachers can go to educational Web sites (such as www.teachertube.com) and view free professional development videos.

You can also foster professional growth by using your school-based inservice days as opportunities to conduct high-quality, self-designed, and self-maintained staff development. At Falls Church High School in Falls Church, Virginia, we were part of a staff development committee whose purpose was to review current literature on instruction, assessment, methodologies, and other topics related to educational practice. We used our findings to develop proposals for the leadership team's consideration, and topics were selected for each inservice day as the year progressed.

Committee members provided training, shared information, and led demonstrations showing how they had applied new strategies in their own classrooms. This model of staff development was facilitated by leaders but owned by the staff. The school conducted these inservices with little to no expense (other than procuring such instructional supplies as poster paper, markers, overhead transparencies, and other materials found in most schools' supply rooms). After the first year, teachers who were not on the committee started suggesting topics of interest to research. With a focus on increasing the quality—not the quantity—of inservice days, this staff's interest in and enthusiasm for staff development increased significantly.

Encourage Sharing Across Departments and Grade Levels

Some schools persist with the notion that teachers can only learn from and support colleagues who teach the same subject. Yet schools that don't encourage buildingwide collaboration and dialogue risk graduating students who define knowledge as discrete facts and growing teachers who take limited advantage of the resources at their disposal. Cross-curricular thinking and sharing is essential for schools and students to succeed. For example, one school that earned poor scores on the state's English objectives on reading and interpreting directions and technical information developed ways for the entire staff to improve student performance. Music teachers had students write directions on the proper way to clean musical equipment, art teachers had students write directions on how to prepare the kiln for firing pottery, and so on. In each class, students read and followed directions to determine their accuracy and, as a result, were able to relate the importance of directions to all aspects of life.

When science teachers in another school found that students were not performing well in the area of human anatomy, they enlisted the help of health and physical education teachers. When students ran relays in gym class, instead of passing a baton they placed Velcro-backed felt organs on human silhouettes on the other side of the gym; students received credit for the run only if they correctly placed the organ. This particular lesson used five of Armstrong's (2000) "eight ways of learning" (p. 22). Armstrong suggests that when teachers deliver new information in a variety of learning styles, the new knowledge will endure over time and be more readily available for retrieval. The above interdisciplinary lesson is a result of an Action Learning Program (Marquardt, 1999, pp. 133–134). Figure 3.1, adapted from Marquadt's concept of Action Learning, depicts one method for framing cross-departmental sharing.

These cross-departmental initiatives are effective and even enjoyable, but they won't happen by chance. It's up to you, as a leader, to provide direction and coordinate such learning opportunities at faculty meetings and inservice days.

Figure 3.1	Action Learning Program
Action Steps	**What Does It Look Like?**
Place individuals in unfamiliar settings.	The physical education teacher attends science department meetings.
Discuss areas that need improvement.	Students are not doing well on state science assessments.
Look at things through a different lens.	Physical education class complements science instruction.
Unfreeze and reshape underlying assumptions.	Physical education is not limited to health, athletics, and exercise.
Reassess programmed knowledge and replace it with new knowledge.	Redesign the organization of running relay exercises.
Review and reflect on feedback that leads to professional growth.	Investigate other opportunities to complement different instructional programs.

Support Collaboration Efforts

Leaders frequently ask us whether it is OK to allow a staff member who is unwilling to meet with others or who is noncompliant in professional discussions to opt out of meetings. Our response is quite straightforward: we do not support negotiating an exemption for any staff. Doing so communicates that you do not hold all staff members to the same standard. Teachers may think that you don't believe their exempt colleagues can grow professionally or offer anything to others. Holding all teachers to the same expectations and standards is simply respectful. Therefore, it is essential that you support your teachers' collaboration efforts by ensuring that they all participate on some level.

You do need to talk with teachers who present concerns about their collaboration. A common complaint is that collaborating or attending these meetings is a waste of time, especially with everything else they have to do. This charge can open the door to a conversation about what is really going on in the meetings. In some cases, you might discover that members are having difficulty functioning as a team; a lack of focus and an inability to communicate effectively greatly diminish teachers' efficacy and lead to frustration and resentment.

Sometimes it takes a while for teachers to realize how advantageous collaboration can be. For example, in a large Southern California high school where teachers were concerned about their planning time being consumed by collaboration, one teacher's bell ringer practices helped them understand the value of collaborating. This teacher's bell ringers consisted of five questions shown on timed PowerPoint slides. The moment the tardy bell rang, the first question appeared. After 15 seconds, the first question disappeared and then the next one came up, and so on. By connecting his bell ringers to a timer, the teacher maximized learning time and focused his students' energy. After his colleagues discovered his technique, they agreed that it was something they would like to incorporate in their own classrooms. However, they immediately identified the amount of time it would take to create the Power-Point as an obstacle and abandoned the idea. It took one of the teachers a couple of minutes to point out that the original teacher had already constructed the PowerPoint template. This was the purpose of collaboration: why should all of them create that file when it was already done? That was the first step. They soon realized that collaboration enabled them to do all kinds of things in a more structured setting and with a more concentrated, efficient approach, including

- Discussing new ideas.
- Trading strategies and tips.
- Identifying essential knowledge and skills.
- Examining and adjusting the curriculum when necessary.
- Problem solving.
- Supporting new teachers.
- Establishing goals.
- Reviewing student work.
- Designing activities and assessments.
- Analyzing data.
- Completing administrative tasks.
- Reading and studying professional materials.
- Conducting administrative observations and walk-throughs.

Conduct Administrative Observations

Administrative observations become much easier to conduct when teachers have a shared understanding of what constitutes best practices in the classroom. If this has not happened, the shared leadership team needs to begin engaging in these discussions as a group, then in the team members' respective departments, and then as a whole faculty (see Resource 10). The result of this process will be that you have a list of expectations that were developed for teachers by teachers. When you conduct observations as an administrator, you are supporting the staff's collective commitment to a quality educational environment.

It's a good idea to have the principal evaluate all first-year teachers. There are several benefits to this. First, the principal will be modeling what he or she values, which develops a consistent set of standards throughout the building. Assistant principals in particular will appreciate seeing firsthand what is expected from observations and evaluations. Working with first-year staff also helps keep principals' evaluation skills fresh and demonstrates that they are willing and able to do the hard work they expect of their administrative staff.

In the case of an ineffective teacher who needs additional time and attention, walk-throughs (see Resource 11) can provide additional data. We certainly want to help teachers improve, but we must also be upfront in recognizing when an ineffective teacher is unwilling or incapable of improvement. In these instances, walk-throughs conducted by teacher leaders or administrators can provide information that will be needed to follow an extraction route.

Extraction is an indication that the teacher is not a good match for his or her current position. If you come across a teacher who is incapable of being helped or of seeing the need to change, he or she needs to be counseled to another position. Still, we don't recommend rushing into extraction mode without first building a solid foundation of objective information and supports. We rarely find teachers who are struggling because they are making a conscious choice not to do well; often, they don't know how to do better. It is almost always easier to help a teacher improve than to remove him or her and hire a new teacher.

Walk-throughs are beneficial because they provide immediate feedback to teachers. The more frequently you conduct walk-throughs, the more they become a norm for the school, and the less obtrusive they will be. If you conduct them on an occasional basis, teachers may believe that you are looking for negative "gotcha" moments rather than trying to help them grow and learn. Regular walk-throughs instill instructional values and strategies to help teachers grow as professionals and support the school's vision. They also enable you to recognize your staff for its efforts and expertise and to catch *positive* "gotcha" moments. They are a great resource for the "Smiles" strategy we mentioned earlier in the chapter.

Walk-throughs are also a quick and easy way to remain aware of what is occurring in your building instructionally. When parents call to complain about something in their child's class, it is nice to be able to state that you have recently been in that classroom. This tells the parents that you are engaged and aware of what's going on with your teachers and classrooms, and it also furnishes you with the firsthand knowledge to discuss specific issues.

Bringing Out the Best in Your Staff

Getting the most out of your staff is not easy, but it is an essential component to helping your team, department, or school thrive. You have to work with all the people in your building, and collaboration is a great way not only to help teachers learn and grow but also to bolster the weaker areas of your staff. Ultimately, school improvement is not about him, or her, or you; it is about getting better for the sake of all students. Some teachers will balk at this notion of change, but they need to accept that their main purpose should be helping their students—the principal stakeholders of any school.

Getting Started

- Demonstrate value for staff members and display enthusiasm, patience, and respect.
- Discuss the benefits of collaborative planning.
- Lead staff in developing common formative assessments.
- Make meaningful observations—by both peers and administrators—part of the culture.

4

Helping Students Succeed

It has become fashionable for schools to proclaim that they hold high expectations for their students. Especially in the current era of accountability, touting high expectations is often read as a sign that progress is occurring, reassuring parents and gratifying politicians.

A large body of research indicates that high expectations have a positive influence on student achievement (Bamburg, 1994; Bui, 2007). Most educators are familiar with some version of the story of the classroom teacher who treated underachieving students as honors students, expecting higher-level work from them than anyone else ever had. The students rose to the occasion, performing as well as or better than the "official" honors students. The teacher's strategy of merely asking more from students led the students to surpass all expectations.

Many teachers do have high expectations. They believe that their students are capable of success, regardless of race, religion, gender, sexual orientation, or socioeconomic status. They see potential in all their students and strive to help them recognize and reach this potential. Yet some teachers don't know how to communicate their expectations to students and are frustrated when students fail to rise to those expectations. And, of course, there are those teachers who have low expectations, which they convey to their students, whether actively or passively. Some of these teachers are apathetic, simply collecting their paychecks and trying not to rock the boat. Others unleash unabashed skepticism and cynicism in the faculty lounge.

As a school leader, you need to keep in mind that teachers' expectations—high, low, or nonexistent—will have a profound effect on their students. You may not be able to immediately convert those teachers who have low expectations. Having high expectations sounds easy but can actually involve difficult, draining work that not all educators want to engage in. The best thing you can do is firmly ingrain high expectations in the building's culture and phase out teachers whose values and practices fail to align with the culture.

Students will rise to meet high expectations. You just need to provide support to help them reach their destination.

Demonstrate High Expectations

It's not immediately clear what *high expectations* really means. Vague and ubiquitous, the phrase can come across as a hocus-pocus incantation: vow that you will have high expectations, wave your wand, and your students will magically achieve more. Of course, this is a bit of an exaggeration, but what does having high expectations really entail? The following sections describe ways both to express high expectations and to hold students accountable to those expectations. They will not strain your school's budget, yet they have the potential to yield extraordinary results.

Express Confidence in Your Students

Expressing confidence and faith in students lies at the core of high expectations. Any adult in the building who says "I believe in you" to a student conveys high expectations. Students need to hear this message regularly. For example, in one school where we worked, the administration supplied the staff with "glad notes," or postcards from the school's supply budget that teachers could write encouraging words on and send to students. They might congratulate students on a test, praise them for their effort on an assignment, or compliment them on their performance in a competition. Above all, the teachers were specific in what they highlighted.

The postcards carried more weight than verbal praise because they were thoughtful and purposeful. Anyone can say something in passing, but deliberately going out of one's way to handwrite a note means more. Because the sentiment was written down, it also allowed students to savor and digest what teachers had said while serving as a future reminder and motivator. These simple deeds are important because they can lead students to think, "Well, if my teacher believes in me, then maybe I should believe in me as well!" Once students start thinking that they are capable of success, they feel a sense of self-esteem and efficacy—that regardless of uncontrollable outside factors, they can exert some level of control over their future.

Establish Rapport

To be vocal, supportive, and encouraging of your students, you need to establish a rapport with them. Sometimes teachers get so caught up in the stresses of administrative tasks like planning, grading, and communicating with parents that they forget the power of building rapport. You should remind your staff members from time to time in postobservation conferences, e-mails, and faculty meetings about the importance of rapport and discuss ways to develop it. An easy but powerful way to establish a connection with kids is to take an interest in their hobbies, extracurricular lives, and likes and dislikes. Even though we log long hours in our demanding jobs, we should find the time to attend choral concerts, basketball games, forensics competitions, and club meetings (even those we don't share an interest in). Many students will respect you more for attending something they are involved in than for your content knowledge and teaching expertise. One teacher we know makes a point to attend an extracurricular event that each of his students participates in and to approach each student involved after the event or during the next school day to discuss some aspect of it. He specifically references something that the student did well or asks a question that allows the student to share his or her knowledge.

Another way to build rapport is simply to talk with students outside the classroom. Encourage your teachers to stop for a moment as they pass through the cafeteria, for example, and ask a student how his or her day is going so far. Just chatting with a student about the school lunch is more social interaction than some students have with their peers all day long. You might greet students on their way into the building in the morning or send them off at the end of the day, modeling to your teachers how they can do the same in their classrooms. Sometimes it is this simple touch that makes a real difference in the lives of students.

Help your teachers understand that establishing rapport can make other aspects of their job easier.

We know a middle school math teacher who begins every year by inviting her students to bring in pictures of their pets or, if they don't have pets, a picture of a pet they would like to have. She then posts the photos with the students' names underneath on a bulletin board. Animals are an easy conversation starter with most children, but the activity doesn't have to be limited to pets; teachers could ask students to bring in photos of anything from their lives that they could share with the class. The point of the activity is to establish a positive classroom environment and a student–teacher relationship that goes beyond the curriculum.

Another great way to establish rapport is simply to learn students' names. This sounds obvious, but we have encountered numerous teachers who address their students impersonally or who can't seem to remember a student's name in discussions with colleagues. Just for a moment, imagine how you would feel about a supervisor who doesn't know your name. How motivated would you be to work for that supervisor—to meet his or her expectations? Model your expectations of your teachers by learning as many of the students' names in your school as possible.

When we were teachers, we would set aside class time on the first day of school every year to learn the names of our students. Through team- and trust-building activities, we discovered that we were able to build an immediate sense of community in our classrooms. During the evenings of those first days, we would study the school yearbook. One teacher we knew learned students' names before school even started and personalized seating cards for them, calling her classroom the 9th Grade Café. Such practices promote community and student buy-in and build mutual respect.

Encourage teachers to create and share relationship-building strategies.

. . . .

Students are more inclined to work for someone who cares about them—not as a statistic or a piece of demographic data but as a person with real feelings, hopes, and aspirations. If your teachers are able to develop a strong rapport with their students, students will be more likely to work toward your teachers' high expectations.

Respect and Challenge Your Students

Don't let your teachers fall prey to the Willy Loman syndrome: it is definitely more important for students to respect them than to like them. If you meet with your novice teachers before the school year starts, be sure to make this one of your talking points. Too many teachers try to build friendships instead of strong student–teacher relationships, failing to see the difference. Students look to us for leadership, guidance, and support, regardless of what they might communicate; to act like a friend in an effort to buy respect almost always has disastrous results.

One teacher we knew worked very hard at being liked by her students instead of respecting and challenging them. Her rules were lax, and her classroom lacked structure. For example, she would often lend her car keys to students to go pick up coffee during the school day, which sent the message that her instruction wasn't important. This didn't build positive rapport or foster academic rigor, and her juvenile perspective ultimately led to a student physically hurting himself. This is obviously an extreme example, but we're sure you could identify a few teachers in your building who don't challenge (or, by extension, respect) their students.

Other teachers try to bargain with students: "I'll give you easy work and leave you alone if you behave and don't bother me." These deals insult students and ultimately rarely work. The students might enjoy the pacts for a while, but they eventually grow bored and resentful.

Classroom deals can have an adverse ripple effect throughout the building.

In fact, in our experience, behavioral problems usually increase as a result of such agreements; the students lose respect for teachers so willing to negotiate away their authority and can find no meaning or relevance in the simple work they receive, so as a result begin acting out in class.

Be sure to emphasize these points during faculty meetings and postobservation conferences because some teachers think they are doing their students a favor by being lax. You may need to explain that the greatest favor teachers can pay is to give appropriate, challenging work and hold students accountable for it.

Question the Existence of "General" Classes

Some schools are dissolving basic, or general, classes—leveled core classes that are below regular classes. Proponents of general classes argue that they are necessary because their enrollees are less capable and need more help in mastering skills and content than others. Although these students may need extra attention, however, they are not necessarily less capable than their peers.

Students generally perform as they are expected to perform, and general classes set the bar very low. Schools also often use these classes as a dumping ground for students with disciplinary problems. Even more disheartening is that new teachers—those who are the least experienced and equipped to deal effectively with such classes—are usually assigned to teach them because they have to "pay their dues."

If general classes were dissolved and the students were dispersed across the regular classes, there probably would not be more than two "problem" students in any given class. In our experience, this integration does not hurt the classroom environment. Peer pressure to conform has a remarkable effect, and because the problem students have lost their audience, the number of referrals to the main office usually drops. In addition, when presented with more challenging work, students generally rise to the occasion. In fact, all some of these students needed was engaging and applicable work. Skillful teachers are able to differentiate their instruction to help all students succeed in the integrated environment.

The notion of eliminating general classes is not always well received by teachers. It often means that they must make changes in their instruction or classroom management. Veteran staff members who believe they have already "done their time" with these students are particularly resistant because they see only what they have to lose. If you do decide to eliminate these classes, explain in advance what will happen and explain the benefits of doing so. It might help to solicit "testimonials" from teachers of general classes who can confirm that their students have both needs and potential, are grateful for instruction, and are enjoyable to teach (sometimes more so than the "good" kids).

Show Them What High Expectations Look Like

Simply telling our students that we expect a lot from them won't sufficiently motivate them. One of our favorite lines when we were teachers was "Show me, don't tell me!" We believe that teachers as well as students should be held to this. So encourage your teachers to show their students exactly what they expect and what they think their students can do. Teachers should use both class-created and teacher-constructed rubrics that clearly detail what an *A* product looks like, and so on. Examples of past products or anchors further enable students to visualize and understand expectations.

You should also encourage teachers to display student work if they don't already. You can initiate this by decorating the main office with student artwork. Student displays communicate school expectations, foster students' and teachers' pride in student work, enhance the overall school environment, and represent the school well to visitors.

Accept Only the Acceptable

As much as we profess to have high expectations, our actions sometimes convey the opposite. When we ignore unacceptable work or behavior, we are lowering our expectations. When we remain silent, we tacitly communicate consent. Unacceptable behaviors are just as contagious as acceptable ones, and they can have a significant negative effect on the learning environment. If we want students to accept our larger expectations, we need to enforce and follow up on the smaller ones.

The guiding philosophy we inherited from a former principal was simple: "If you wouldn't want it pictured or written about in the *Washington Post*, then why allow it to continue?" This kind of thinking has broad and powerful implications. For example, it is easy for a teacher to overlook a student who comes to class tardy unexcused if it's by just a minute. If

Address inappropriate behavior to avoid systemic growth of poor behaviors among staff and students.

we see the student coming down the hall, why not just let it slide? But imagine that a few days later, the student is five minutes late. A week later, a handful of students are piled up outside the door arriving late. No teacher would want this behavior highlighted in the media. Once you ignore one student's behavior, you open the door for others to engage in the same behavior because you have silently conveyed the message that it is acceptable.

The same holds true when it comes to academics. For example, some content-area teachers accept work with poor grammar or spelling because they lack self-confidence or expertise in that area. In one high school meeting we attended with teachers of multiple academic disciplines, staff members discussed the fact that students experienced varying levels of expectations depending on the teacher or content area. The teachers agreed that if they saw errors in any area—spelling, grammar, math, and so on—they would at least call them to the student's attention. They would not necessarily deduct points from the grade, but they decided that they had an obligation to communicate to the student that some aspect of the work was unacceptable and needed to be fixed. By not doing so before, the teachers were conveying that mediocre work was acceptable in that content area or program. These lowered expectations also reinforced the notion that elements of language arts were important only in an English classroom, that math mattered only to math teachers, and so on.

When students submit work that is beneath their abilities, effective teachers return it to the students and expect them to improve it. When students fare poorly on a test, effective teachers have them work on the areas they performed poorly on. Effective teachers also call parents regularly to update them on students' progress and to enlist their help in maintaining high expectations (getting their children to turn in missing work, for example). "Good enough" is, quite simply, not good enough.

Help Them Own the Answers

Some of the best teachers we have observed are the ones who are sometimes reluctant to answer student questions. Good teachers don't always make knowledge acquisition easy because they want their students to *own* the answer, not simply *receive* the answer.

Often, teachers' first impulse when asked a question is to answer it; to many, supplying answers is what makes one a teacher.

But this is not a full or accurate picture. A good teacher is one who helps students acquire the necessary knowledge and skills themselves. By not immediately answering questions, teachers send the message that they believe students are capable of finding a solution on their own. By readily supplying answers, a teacher may unintentionally send signals of "I don't think you're capable of doing this on your own." You might want to look for this kind of behavior during classroom observations and discuss it during conferences with your teachers.

Employ Cooperative Learning

If we as educators try to pinpoint when we really learned to teach, we would probably say that we became professional educators once we actually began teaching on our own; we didn't become experts until we became practitioners. The same holds true for students. So it makes sense for our students to work with, learn from, and teach one another. Lecturing is not just the strategy of teachers who don't know any other way; it is also the tool of those who don't trust their students to learn on their own. In contrast, cooperative learning makes students part of the learning process.

A cooperative learning environment encourages students to make the most of their strengths and help others in their areas of weakness. Once students have worked together to reach solutions, they have an opportunity to present their findings to the rest of the class. This helps build students' sense of efficacy and demonstrates the teacher's high expectations. Cooperative learning can be a significant cultural change for teachers not used to giving this responsibility and opportunity to their students, so you need to emphasize the importance of using this strategy and reinforce it with your teachers when possible.

Give Feedback

When we talk about feedback, we're referring not only to what occurs in the classroom and in conferences but also to detailed written feedback that students can digest later. Our students may be young, but they too have many distractions and issues in their lives that make it easy for them to forget the details. Students need consistent, timely, specific feedback on their progress and on their weaker areas.

If we're willing to accept it, feedback is our friend. When you provide it, be as specific as possible.

As an analogy, picture a golf team that practices once a week at the driving range. As is correct, the players keep their heads down while they swing and don't always see where or how far out their balls land, although they have some idea. After a few weeks of practice, the coach provides the team members with detailed feedback—the number of times they hit the fairway, how often they were slicing or drawing their shots, and so on. These are good data for a golfer to have. The problem is that the data are not *timely*. The players spent weeks repeating and reinforcing the same mistakes. It would take a considerable amount of time for team members to break and correct old habits—but a very short amount of time for them to become disengaged and frustrated with both their lack of growth and the game. How helpful would this be to a team's success? Not very. This is why good coaches provide frequent feedback in manageable, timely chunks.

At one middle school we worked at, the shared leadership team agreed that it would benefit students, parents, and teachers to provide all students with a grade at the end of each week, as though they were withdrawing from the school and transferring to another. This increased feedback enabled students to monitor their grades more closely and identify what they needed to do to improve. In addition, delivering accurate paper grades to each student on a weekly basis was a good measure of teachers' self-discipline. If you want to see what kind of school you have, pop into your workrooms and classrooms at the close of the marking period on a teacher work day: are teachers scrambling to grade work and enter grades into their gradebooks, or are they analyzing data, mapping out curriculum, and planning instruction? Your observations will tell you a lot about what goes on in your classrooms.

Feedback does not have to exclude criticism, as long as it is given in a positive manner. Constructive criticism builds respect and actually demonstrates caring for students. If a student demonstrates behavior that warrants criticism, then ignoring the behavior can be misconstrued as accepting or even condoning the behavior. When approached in a positive and caring way, students—like adults—can use criticism to improve and control their own growth.

Acknowledge and Examine Stereotypes, Biases, and Prejudices

Stereotypes, biases, and prejudices are silent destroyers. Socially unacceptable and inappropriate beliefs can be very uncomfortable to discuss with even the closest of peers, but we all know they exist. Our suggestion is to acknowledge that we all have different beliefs and preferences and then to assess whether our values are standing in the way of building and maintaining productive, positive relationships with our students.

In one faculty meeting, we brought this to the surface by asking staff members if anyone wanted to share his or her prejudices with the group. The silence was uncomfortable. Some teachers stared in disbelief, while others nervously scanned the room to see whether anyone would actually speak up. After a reasonable amount of wait time, we suggested that most of us are prejudiced to a certain degree: for example, some of us are biased against older drivers; others, against younger drivers.

We used this introduction to lead into a larger issue. We know teachers who study their class rosters during the inservice days before the school year begins and make comments like, "Look at my class list. I guess I know what my year is going to be like." Just looking at the names, these teachers make some quick assumptions about their students' ability levels, attitudes, and behavior. For example, some teachers assume that female students will underperform in math class. Many of these teachers lower their expectations before they even welcome their students into the classroom, setting the tone for the year before the first bell even rings. This kind of behavior is inexcusable, but it is prevalent.

Challenge yourself by looking closely at your own biases, and then make a plan for adjustment.

· · · · · · · · · · · · · · · · · · · ·

One way to address and overcome such stereotyping is to present your staff with specific research that refutes their prejudices and open up a dialogue. For example, you might provide math teachers with literature that debunks certain notions about gender and achievement. *Girls Are . . . Boys Are . . . : Myths, Stereotypes and Gender Differences* (Campbell & Storo, 1994) is a good resource to share, for example. You might also share vignettes or data from *90-90-90 schools*, a term created by Douglas Reeves (2000) to describe schools where 90 percent of students come from a minority background, 90 percent of students are eligible for free or reduced-price lunch, and 90 percent of students meet state standards. We don't celebrate schools like these enough, especially because the media focus far more on schools that do not meet standards. So debunk myths and illustrate the power of expectations, but first get the issue on the table for discussion and ask staff to identify ways to reduce stereotyping and prejudice in the building.

Involve Students as Partners in the Classroom

Involving students as partners in the classroom demonstrates our trust and respect in them and reflects their value as active citizens of the school and, to a broader extent, society. Just as the family that works together stays together (Covey, 1997), the classroom that works together succeeds together. It is crucial to include students in our practice as much as possible. Here are some ways to do that.

Develop Rules Together. All classrooms have rules. Although some rules are not negotiable, most have some flexibility. For example, Northwood High School in Montgomery County, Maryland, had a policy that students late to class must be documented and that each teacher is responsible for disciplining the tardy students. That's the nonnegotiable part; the negotiable part is what happens when a student is late. One teacher at this school told his class that he valued student input, briefly discussed possible consequences and procedures, and then recorded several ideas from the students to address the infraction.

In a short time, the students helped develop a policy and a process: each week, the teacher wrote a list of days on the board when he would be available for students serving detention or needing additional time and support. Next, the class developed a form for tardy students to complete when they arrived to class late. On the form, they would fill in their name, the date, and the time and note whether the tardy was excused or unexcused. If it was unexcused, they needed to pick a date from the board to serve detention; if it was excused, they needed to put the excuse note in a basket near the door. If a student caught a classmate not signing in for a detention, the student with the infraction was automatically assigned two detentions: one for being tardy and the other for not following tardy procedures. This process was designed almost entirely by the students. Within just a couple of months, tardiness decreased in this class. Because students felt ownership of the rules, they consequently followed them very well.

Elect a Greeter. In the same class we just described, the students were learning a trade, and part of the curriculum included learning personal presentation skills. The teacher decided to assign a different student each week to be the classroom greeter. When someone came to the door, the greeter would meet the visitor, shake hands, and introduce him- or herself by name and title as the greeter for the classroom. The greeter would then ask the visitor what brought him or her to the class and how the greeter could be of assistance. This procedure allowed the teacher to continue teaching with minimal interruptions and helped the students develop interpersonal skills and a sense of classroom community.

Enlist "Teachers." Once students have mastered a particular skill, teachers can recruit them as secondary teachers. We knew one multilevel classroom in which third-year students were required to mentor first-year students. This setup required first- and second-year students to go to third-year students for assistance before going to the teacher. This practice afforded the teacher more time to focus on areas of need in the program and honed the mentors' teaching skills as well as reinforcing their own knowledge of the skill or content taught. Finally, the policy cemented the importance of succeeding as a class, not simply as individuals.

Solicit Input. Students are a wealth of information; we just have to ask for it sometimes. Ask your teachers to have their students evaluate how class went for the week or the day. Several effective teachers we know hand out index cards on Friday, asking students to write "well" on one side and "not as well" on the other. Students then list at least one item for each side of the card—something that went well that week and something that didn't go as well. At first, students were reluctant to write anything that wasn't positive, but once their teachers were able to instill and demonstrate trust, they provided good feedback for classroom adjustments.

Another way your teachers can solicit student input is to administer student surveys (see Resource 12). We have found it helpful to invite another teacher in to distribute and collect the surveys so that students truly feel that their responses are anonymous. When students feel that they can share how they believe their learning is going or provide input on how things should progress, they gain a greater sense of ownership of their education and their classroom. One caveat: Sometimes the student responses may sound cruel. Remind your teachers that the students may just be being brutally honest, or they may be trying to get their teachers riled. Sometimes sharing the responses with the class helps squelch future inappropriate responses. In addition, teachers' willingness to go public with negative as well as positive feedback models the important trait of humility and demonstrates that they have high expectations of themselves as well as students.

Support Your Students

High expectations unaccompanied by support will result in failure and frustration for both students and teachers. Changing your school's culture to one of high expectations requires a two-pronged approach. Thus far we have covered how to demonstrate high expectations; now we discuss how to support learners in fulfilling them.

Help Students Set Goals

Most students do not know what it takes to set and achieve goals. For example, many students claim that they want to be recording artists, but other than saying "I want to rap" or "I want to play the guitar," they don't know how to articulate their goals. They may not have considered that they will need to learn about music theory and history and recording technology, or that running a record label might actually be a better fit, in which case they would need to take business and marketing courses.

Teachers can help by walking students through the goal-setting process. Students should first identify areas of interest and then set an accompanying goal that they would like to achieve in a realistic period of time. Teachers could teach their students about the SMART goals we discussed in Chapter 2. They might complement that with helping them to identify factors and qualities that would help them achieve benchmarks and goals as well as ones that would derail them. All of these actions are helpful because students usually lack the necessary knowledge, the skills required to research their goals, and the understanding of what is involved overall. Teachers can use this goal-setting process as an opportunity to teach students a variety of skills and show how it is applicable in their present academic situation. Finally, be sure to remind your teachers to have periodic goals conferences and check-ins with students.

Reward Achievement and Positive Behavior

Although some research claims that giving rewards for high academic performance and good behavior is detrimental to learning and that students are most motivated by the intrinsic and personal satisfaction of learning, we believe that rewards have their place. As Crystal Kuykendall (2004) explains, "Teachers and administrators must be willing to reward students who fulfill their goals. Students are motivated by rewards; when success is rewarded, it is reinforced" (p. 121). She further notes that "educators must work very hard to dispel the belief that it does not pay to do well academically" (p. 121). After all, the real world works on a kind of reward system. If you show up to work, you receive a paycheck; if you perform exceptionally well, you may receive a financial bonus. Rewards are one way of equipping students for our globally competitive workforce.

Motivation often results from a combination of internal and external factors. It is true that learning and succeeding are gratifying in and of themselves, and we want our students to know and experience this. But rewards can help trigger that appreciation and motivation.

Many schools have some kind of reward system in place. For example, a Good Credit Rewards program, loosely based on principal Dan Parris's Passport System at Rocky Run Middle School in Fairfax, Virginia, is an example of a program you can implement with "little or no money down" (see Resource 13). As with credit cards, students earn "good credit" or reward points through high grades, low absenteeism, and low discipline referrals. Student cardholders start out with "application pending" status and can progress to the silver, gold, and platinum levels, each of which grants the cardholder a certain level of access to school functions and incentives. When students' credit rating is too low for them to participate in certain activities, they work with a teacher assigned to help them improve their status.

One of the biggest benefits of this system is its cost-effectiveness. Most of the rewards are admission to events rather than tangible prizes, so they do not strain the school budget. Your school's student leadership can brainstorm possible rewards and incentives and hold class meetings or survey classmates for suggestions. This component is important because it invites a broad range of collaboration and ownership among the student body. Rewards that come from them will have better staying power than privileges handed down to students. Viable rewards that students commonly suggest include early dismissal for lunch or the school day, exam exemption, homework passes, a field day or picnic, special parking privileges, and preferential lunch seating.

Printing membership cards can be as inexpensive as the rewards themselves. Many yearbook companies print identification cards for students in the schools they have a contract with; it would be easy enough to add a platinum, gold, or silver bar or band on them to designate students' status. Many yearbook companies even donate the printers necessary for these IDs, so schools would be able to print new IDs quarterly to reflect students' progress.

Celebrate Effort

There will always be a segment of students who do not achieve as much as others, no matter how hard they work. It is important to recognize and celebrate those students who make gains or demonstrate genuine effort, regardless of their level of achievement. You could encourage such practices as the aforementioned "glad notes" or incorporate celebrations as part of a rewards program. However you decide to do it, students need to see, hear, and believe that their effort matters. You can provide encouragement by sharing your own personal success stories during grade-level student meetings and suggesting to your teachers that they do the same, or by inviting guest speakers from the community to share their own anecdotes. One teacher we knew incorporated stories of her personal success in the face of adversity and only revealed later that they were about her.

Park View High School in Loudoun County, Virginia, a diverse school with a 40 percent minority student population, has a tradition for celebrating students known as PATS (Patriots Achieving Towards Success) Night. This program honors students who have demonstrated significant effort or improvement in the area of academic achievement. The school hosts a potluck dinner in the cafeteria and an awards ceremony where students listen to a motivational speaker and receive certificates on stage. This evening is one of the school's most popular, highly attended events.

Help Students Take Charge of Their Learning

One of the most effective things teachers can do is let go of some control and help students take ownership of their own learning plans. To put students on this path, teachers should provide students with clear learning expectations and conduct quality formative assessments. As Black and Wiliam (1998) note, formative assessment "yields particularly good results with low achievers by concentrating on specific problems with their work and giving them a clear understanding of what is wrong and how to put it right" (p. 7). Students need to know how they are measuring up to the teacher's expectations, and it might also be helpful to know how they are doing in relation to other students. Once students know where they stand academically, they can identify where they should be and how they are going to get there.

Besides providing students with accurate and easy-to-understand assessment results, you should ensure that they have somewhere to go for specific help. For example, a 5th grade team we know provides students with access to additional support before, during, and after the school day. The team shares responsibility for the entire grade, and the common assessments ensure that students' success does not hinge on seeing their own classroom teachers. The assessment results provide a level of detail that gives any team member a specific focus to help the student. For example, the results for one student might indicate that he or she needs a better understanding of the comparison value of single-digit fractions with different denominators. Common assessment results take the guesswork out of identifying what kind of support students need.

Incorporate Mentoring and Tutoring

In some high schools we know, mentoring a student is an assumed responsibility of each adult in the building. Although such mentoring enhances school culture and student achievement, it does add an additional responsibility to teachers' often-heavy workloads. In addition, many teachers are already informal mentors to their students. It might therefore be more feasible—and equally powerful—to design and implement a student mentoring program.

Many schools are making gains in student achievement by having high-performing students mentor their peers. Your school probably already has certain groups from which you can pull these potential mentors. Look at your master schedule and the list of clubs and organizations, and enlist the assistance of teachers and sponsors. For example, honor societies and social science courses often require community service, and mentoring or tutoring other students may count toward this requirement. Having students support their peers in this way automatically gives students greater ownership of their school's learning culture. Mentoring programs are easy to implement and can be student-directed under the guidance of the honor society's faculty advisor. In one district we know, the high school's National Honor Society provides tutors and mentors to students at its feeder middle school, whose National Junior Honor Society in turn provides tutors and mentors to its feeder elementary schools. This kind of program can easily be coordinated through a spreadsheet that tracks time spent working with students.

Another cost-effective model would be to invite business partners to come in and work with students. At the high school level, you might approach your business and marketing teachers to identify interested volunteers among their community contacts. Many professionals in the business world want to give something

Be sure to incorporate community resources. Work with your staff to reach out to the community. And remember that your staff are the residents, spouses, neighbors, and friends of the community.

. . . .

back to the community in addition to, or instead of, simply making a deposit into the school's bank account. People enjoy sharing their knowledge and interests, so many business partners jump at the chance to work with students—and positively influence potential future business colleagues.

Turn Consequences into Meaningful Time

When students violate school rules, they often expect consequences. Typical consequences at the secondary school level include detention, in-school suspension, Saturday school detention, and out-of-school suspension. When possible, we suggest finding ways to convert these consequences into learning opportunities. This will help students understand that you are not just looking for ways to punish them but that you are also concerned about their academic well-being. Many of the students who frequent the administrator's office are also experiencing academic difficulties.

We created a new detention policy reflecting this purpose at Falls Church High School in Falls Church, Virginia. Under the old policy, students were given the date of detention, the room number, the amount of time to serve, and the accompanying rules (e.g., no talking or sleeping). Students silently served their sentence while a staff member monitored the detention room. We decided to transform this time into an opportunity for students to seek academic assistance from their teachers.

First, we created an incentive for students to seek this extra assistance by doubling the standard consequence of one hour of detention to two hours of detention. Students receiving consequences were offered the opportunity to exchange two hours of detention for one hour of academic help. Students who chose this option were given a form to track the amount of time they spent with their teacher outside of routine class time (see Resource 14). Some students spent their hour with one teacher, while others divided the hour among a few teachers. If a student chose to take advantage of this program, it was his or her responsibility to find times when the teacher was available. The structure that the new policy provided enabled students to take more charge of their learning.

The obvious question here is, How do you keep teachers after school if you are unable to pay them? As much as we try to respect teacher contract time, there are always going to be teachers who come to school early or who like to stay late. You might also consider offering teachers who have the last period of the day as their planning time the chance to come in early to remediate students and allow them to leave early, and vice versa for those who are off during the first block of the day. Students who have study hall or who work as office helpers during the day could also use those periods to seek additional help.

Our new detention policy was a considerable improvement over the old one. Teachers reported that many of their hard-to-reach students made more room in their schedules for additional time and support. Administrators became more involved in their students' academic success instead of simply doling out consequences. In fact, any time a student was called to an administrator's office for discipline reasons, the conversation always began with, "How are your grades?" and "How is your attendance?" Administrators started to assess the areas in which students needed help as well as addressing behavioral problems.

Another practice we implemented with positive results was offering reverse suspensions to parents for less serious disciplinary incidents (e.g., chronic skipping). When students are suspended, parents often complain about having to take off work to supervise their children. But if it's unavoidable, why not have them join their children in school and monitor their attendance, behavior, and completion of work? Parents of older students in particular tend to be concerned about their children's discipline records showing out-of-school suspensions and are thus open to alternatives, even if it means adjusting their schedules.

We provided parents with specific guidelines for their own behavior during the reverse suspensions. For example, they were required to remain attached to their children throughout the day, accompanying them to class, in the halls, and to lunch; they were not permitted to engage their children's teachers in any discussion that would interfere with instructional time; and they were asked to leave their cell phones behind, or at least put them on silent mode.

In addition to keeping students in school and lowering the suspension rate, reverse suspensions provided many unanticipated, beneficial outcomes. The parents gained a better understanding of the internal dynamics of the school and its classrooms, developed an appreciation for the teachers' hard work, and saw how their children were academically challenged throughout the school day. Some teachers commented that having parents in their rooms actually raised the level of their lesson plans for the day. We did not intend the policy to affect teachers' preparation, so this outcome prompted a discussion on why we would perform our responsibilities differently when another adult is in the room.

Before implementing such a policy, it is of course vital to involve teachers in its planning and development. When we created the new policy at Falls Church High School, we sought and obtained buy-in by first reaching an agreement that we needed to improve the routine discipline plan of removing students from sound instructional environments and then deciding how we could turn consequences into meaningful instructional time.

The Power of Expectations

Although it might seem clichéd, we would like to conclude this chapter by highlighting the success of famed math teacher Jaime Escalante. An immigrant to the United States, he had a powerful impact on students in his largely poor and Hispanic high school during the late 1970s and 1980s.

Although we don't want to minimize his instruction or gloss over the fact that it took him years of hard work to build his program and achieve his results—contrary to the image that Hollywood has broadcast—what we want to emphasize here are the expectations he had for his students. He believed that all of his students, regardless of their backgrounds, were capable of succeeding in Advanced Placement (AP) Calculus, a rigorous, highly accelerated college-level class culminating in a national standardized test. He expected nothing less from his students than what he gave them. He refused to settle for "good enough," he communicated his belief in his students, and he showed them that he cared. Student participation and pass rates on the AP exam at Escalante's school rivaled those of nearby academies and advantaged schools (Jessness, 2002). The common denominator of Escalante's story and other similarly inspirational ones is having high expectations for students—and for *ourselves.*

We are confident that you can brainstorm other ways to support and demonstrate high expectations for your students. We urge you to talk with colleagues about their practices in this area. How do you go about finding the time in an already busy day to do so? As you will read in the next chapter, it is not as difficult as you might think.

Getting Started

* Dedicate time at a staff meeting to hear how teachers define high expectations.

* Lead a discussion about expectations as they relate to race, gender, and socioeconomic status.

* Brainstorm ways to demonstrate high expectations and support students.

5

Making the Most
of Your Time

From secretaries to superintendents, newcomers to veterans, everyone in the education field could benefit from having more time. The time investment required to be an educator—for both the challenging and important aspects of our jobs and the basic and mundane ones—is overwhelming. Often, our profession seems like a Sisyphean task of accomplishing more and more with less and less time. As people asking you to change your school, we sympathize. Education is a difficult enough business without being asked to do things differently than they have been done before.

As a leader, your time is valuable, and you would be hard-pressed to make even more happen in an already tight day. Still, although time is a fixed entity, you do have some control over how you use it. In this chapter, we describe strategies that will help you maximize the time you do have.

Manage Your E-Mail

Ever since e-mail has become one of our principal modes of communication, it has also become one of the biggest drains on our time. Managing e-mail involves not just reading and responding to messages but also cleaning out and organizing folders. It is very easy to drown in e-mail. So an important way to maximize your time is to create a system for your e-mail. Organize your inbox so that the most recent e-mails appear at the top, set up folders for saving important e-mails, and create and store templates for standard e-mails that you send often. If your e-mail system has a preview pane, glance at the first few lines of each e-mail rather than opening and reading them all as they come in, then sort them into folders that you rank by priority for responding. Be sure to create folders for subject areas and responsibilities that you regularly deal with so that locating important saved e-mails is not a time-consuming process. Consider setting aside 10 minutes at the start and end of each day to manage e-mail. This is a good way to organize your day and plan for the next one.

Of course, the best way to keep up with your e-mail is to respond to it as it arrives in your in-box. Taking it off your plate right away rather than staring at dozens of messages at the end of the day saves time and reduces stress. Too often, busy leaders delay reading their messages and then suddenly find themselves buried under an avalanche of e-mail, unsure of how to dig their way out.

Another way to maximize time is to set up some ground rules with staff for using e-mail. For example, maybe you don't want every request or piece of information to be sent to you via e-mail, particularly if it could be mentioned to you in person. You might also ask staff members to compose meaningful, specific subject headers for their e-mails that give you the key idea

Control your e-mail— don't let it control you!

. . . .

immediately. You could also state your preference of if and when it is appropriate to be copied on e-mails.

Walk Around

It might sound counterintuitive, but walking around your school can help you get more done more efficiently. If you mentally prepare a list of all the small conversations that you need to have with staff and students and accomplish them on your rounds rather than cornered in your office, your time for other work will increase. You should walk around before school, during instructional periods, in between classes, and even after school.

Engaging in this kind of activity is a variation of what Robbins and Alvy (2004) refer to as Leading and Learning by Walking Around (LLWA). While you walk around, you are certain to learn things about your school's culture that you might not learn seated in front of a computer. Observing staff members, students, and parents in their "natural state" gives you a better feel for what is really happening in your school and sometimes enables you to address issues before they even make it to your office. Consider the following questions as you make your rounds:

- Do students linger in the halls after the tardy bell has rung?
- Do teachers address tardy students?
- Are students in the halls during class without passes?
- Do students congregate at their classroom doors before the dismissal bell has rung?
- What do students carry to class and on their way out of the building?
- What do students talk about in the halls?
- Do teachers help administrators monitor students in the halls between classes, before school, and after school?
- How do staff members talk to students?
- How do students talk to staff members?

- How do teachers treat their duty periods?
- How is curriculum predominantly delivered?
- Where do teachers gather? With whom? What do they discuss?
- What do teachers do with their planning time?

Another benefit of walking around is that you will receive less e-mail. People will learn that it is sometimes easier to grab you and run something by you while you are in the halls than to e-mail you and have to wait for a response. If you norm this practice, you'll find that people will start to seek you out during your travels throughout the building. You should be prepared to address as many issues as you can on these walks, or else you will just be taking a laundry list of things to do with you back to your office. Also, be sure not to roam the building aimlessly, which will just eat up your time. Instead, take purposeful walks, targeting certain areas of the building for specific periods of time. Your visibility and accessibility will build respect and should significantly reduce student and staff problems, which in turn will reduce the amount of time you have to spend in your office.

Categorize and Prioritize

With so much to do in so little time, you need to be organized. In addition to the good old-fashioned to-do list and a smart filing system, a calendar is an obvious must. Most people have some kind of electronic calendar that can be synced to their e-mail. If your district does not have this kind of technology or if purchasing it is cost-prohibitive, a traditional calendar will work almost as well.

You also need to find a way to prioritize your duties. Although labeling and flagging appointments and tasks are helpful, probably the best way to make more time for yourself is to set aside 10 minutes in the morning and afternoon, or whenever you manage your e-mail, to prioritize your tasks. If you are able to start your day with a clear understanding of what needs to be done, what would be nice to get done, and what doesn't need to be done soon, you will have a clearer focus for the day ahead of you.

Keep in mind, however, that life as an educator requires flexibility. Reflect on how often your day does not go as planned. Whether you are blindsided by something, an issue takes longer than expected, or you are needed to cover for a colleague, the best-laid plans often go awry. For that reason, be sure to include some "fluff" in your schedule to account for those unexpected moments that can derail your day. Even if those moments do not happen, you have created more time for yourself to devote to something else.

Learn to Say No

Saying no can be difficult. For the most part, we like to please others and be seen as helpful, so denying a request often generates feelings of guilt. This reluctance to say no is especially sharp in educators, professionals who have sworn to give of themselves and make financial, emotional, and social sacrifices for the betterment of other people's children.

Sometimes you need to step back and ask yourself whether every little detail needs your time and attention. Consider how often you have been in meetings or received e-mails and thought, "You know, I don't have to be here" or "I don't have to be the one to do this." Ideally, we would be able to just say no, but we are so conditioned to take on so much, regardless of whether or not we are able to, that we learn to speak in "apologese" to colleagues. Simply saying "no" causes them to look at us cross-eyed, as though something were wrong with us for not wanting to add more to our plates.

Unfortunately, simply saying that you're too busy to take on something else is not always a good enough reason, because everyone in a school is busy—that is the nature of the job. Instead, you need to cite a specific responsibility that is preventing you from taking on the additional task. You could also ask to think about the request, check your calendar, or talk it over with a colleague first; doing so shows that you gave careful consideration to the request, even if you are unable to accommodate it. If you are reluctant to turn down the request altogether, you could negotiate by saying, "You know, I would love to do that, but I really am unable to; what I *can* do is _____."

Don't feel guilty about saying no and thinking of yourself once in a while—you earned it!

You could also delegate the additional task. Not everything must be done by you. Remember the importance of growing other leaders (see Chapter 1). As long as you are not just passing along grossly undesirable work, find someone who has leadership potential and more flexibility in his or her schedule and who could benefit from the experience, and ask him or her to handle the task instead.

Share Responsibilities

If you are one of several administrators in a school, you may find it helpful to share responsibilities to free one another for additional meetings or to catch up on a backlog of responsibilities. In one medium-sized high school in Maryland with three assistant principals, the discipline problems were escalating and administrators were forced to spend increased amounts of time dealing with them, rendering them unavailable for other responsibilities (especially ones having to do with leadership). With stacks of referrals waiting to be addressed and teachers continuing to send students out of class, the office literally had lines of students outside it from the beginning to the end of the day. It seemed to be an impossible hole to climb out of, especially with other responsibilities hopelessly piling up.

To address the problem, the administrators decided to each take one day a week as a break from discipline issues. On that day, the other two would fill in and handle that administrator's referrals while the administrator engaged in leadership activities (e.g., observing classes) or caught up on other regular responsibilities.

When the administrators returned to their offices after their days off from discipline, they did not have to play catch-up with the previous day's referrals.

This system not only gave the administrators more time to work on other things but also significantly reduced discipline problems: after making this simple scheduling adjustment, the administrators were able to identify and address many causes of the increased student discipline issues because they were able to get out of their offices for longer periods of time. If your school has only one assistant principal, you could use mentees to help with some of the responsibilities (see Chapter 1).

Teach Classroom Management

As obvious as it sounds, the best way to reduce the number of referrals teachers submit is to coach teachers on classroom management strategies. Provide a refresher on such practices as using proximity and mobility in the classroom, devising seating charts, creating class rules, and contacting parents to help you reduce the number of trivial referrals you receive. In addition, here are some valuable talking points for you to discuss with your staff members.

Change Your Approach

Investing time now in sharing management tips and techniques will give you more time later— and make for happier students and teachers.

Many discipline issues escalate because of the way teachers address students. Cornering students will likely cause them to lash out, so discourage your teachers from provoking students, and remind them that the best tactic is always to de-escalate situations. Too often, teachers approach students in this fashion because they feel the need to "win," but confrontations are lose-lose and should be avoided when possible.

In particular, teachers should avoid an audience. No one likes being "called out" in front of friends or colleagues, and students are no exception. Yet many teachers confront students in front of their classmates because they think having an audience will help them. It is therefore understandable, if not condonable, when students talk back to save face in front of their peers. Teachers often exacerbate the situation by demanding that students accompany them to the main office so that they can receive punishment for both their defiance and the infraction that sparked the confrontation.

Instead, teachers should quietly motion students aside to speak with them or find a way to talk privately with them while class members are working independently on a task. Rather than immediately demanding to know why students are not following a certain rule, they should start by asking, "Are you willing to work with me?" or "Could you do me a favor?" This kind of question invites students to work with teachers and demonstrates a more subtle authoritarian tone.

Don't Make Threats You Can't Keep

In the heat of the moment, teachers sometimes make threats they cannot follow up on. Either they do not have the power to enforce their threat, or their ultimatum is a bit too ridiculous to be supported by supervisors. You may have known teachers who told misbehaving students that they would never be allowed back into their class, for example. You can rarely back up these kinds of threats, and they ultimately create more work for you. Before you know it, you have a student sitting outside your office waiting to explain why he was thrown out of class, or a teacher telling you why a student will need to be permanently removed from her class, or an angry parent on hold insisting on an immediate meeting about the situation. Help your teachers understand when you can and cannot support them and how they might avoid making such threats in the future.

Keep Things in Perspective

Some teachers are incredibly rigid and have a hard time working around minor obstacles. For example, a teacher might send a student to the office for forgetting to bring a pen or pencil to class. But how does it help that student academically to sit in an office for 30 minutes, waiting to see an administrator? Encourage teachers to avoid sending students to the office for such small infractions. If the student does not have a pen, then loan him one and ensure through some form of nonvaluable collateral that he returns it at the end of the period.

Other teachers need coaching on not reacting to their "triggers." Some students push their teachers' buttons for a quick and automatic pass to the office: sneezing whenever the teacher is talking, tapping a pencil on the desk—anything that will get under the teacher's skin. Help your teachers understand that this kind of behavior is not personal and that they need to learn to ignore it or not let on that it bothers them. The behavior often continues because students are getting some kind of reward out of it. Explain to your teachers that when they send students out of class for these kinds of minor infractions, not only are they positively reinforcing the behavior, but they are also undermining their own authority in the process.

Some righteously indignant teachers believe that every infraction of every rule must be addressed in the main office. They seem to be seeking some kind of divine justice and an immediate change in behavior and attitude, neither of which is bound to happen through serving detention. Help these teachers understand how tolerance, patience, and understanding can accomplish more in both the short and the long term than a disciplinary consequence.

Hold Standing Meetings

When most people hear the phrase *standing meeting*, they assume that it refers to a regularly occurring meeting on the master calendar. However, here we are literally referring to a meeting where everyone stands. Like in a regular meeting, attendees of a standing meeting congregate, communicate, develop a plan of action, and then take the necessary action—only more quickly. Not all meetings need to be lengthy endeavors. Sometimes an unplanned meeting is necessary, but you can't afford to spend an hour or two sitting around a table.

As the facilitator, you will want to conduct this meeting efficiently. Avoid environments that encourage attendees to relax and socialize. You want their minds sharp, ready to go, and seeking quick closure. If you think this practice sounds odd, consider the standing meetings that coaches hold during games—at the pitcher's mound, on the sidelines of the court, or out of bounds at the 50-yard line. Share this analogy with staff members to stress the feasibility of this kind of meeting.

Find More Time

One of the greatest, and most wasted, resources in schools is time. We cannot overlook the potential of assembling so many highly skilled, highly educated professionals under one roof to help a school thrive. However, in many schools, the inability or lack of motivation to gather these professionals hinders improvement efforts. If we agree that teachers grow by sharing their expertise with colleagues and through the methodical process of data analysis, reflection, and adjustment of their practice, then we must find time for them to meet and collaborate.

Some might view collaboration as a burden, especially when it occurs outside of the contract day at team and department meetings. For teachers who already have a full plate and feel underpaid and underappreciated, meeting with colleagues after work can feel crippling and burdensome. Because the vast majority of educators already selflessly devote

Get ideas from staff members on ways to adjust their current use of time instead of asking them to give more time.

numerous hours of uncompensated time just to meet job expectations and students' needs, it is hard to fault teachers who don't enthusiastically embrace after-hour meetings. But having time to collaborate together can make teachers' jobs and lives easier and can actually give them more time in the long run. To make collaboration a more attractive reality for teachers, then, this team model must be nonintrusive and built into the regular day as much as possible. So investigate ways to create more time for your teachers to work together. You can start by examining the following recommendations.

Schedule Common Time

If you manipulate the master schedule so that teachers of a common subject share the same "free" period, you will be on the road toward creating a culture of collaborative professional development. Giving all English teachers the second period off, for example, would enable them to collaborate during the instructional day without reducing student–teacher contact time. Sounds easy, right? Of course, it does take a little work. In your first attempt to modify the master schedule, you may not be able to do this with all the core areas. If that is the case, use state standardized testing results to assess which areas have the lowest academic achievement and start with those for the first year. This example of data-driven decision making will help you build a foundation and improve test scores.

Help your master schedule builder develop his or her skills by collaborating with other master schedule builders in the district.

The desired cultural shift here is for teachers to *want* time for collaboration with other teachers. Once teachers see their colleagues using common time for professional collaboration in a healthy environment, they will be curious and may hope that their own department or grade level gets the same opportunity. Once you have made these initial inroads, adjustments to the master schedule could receive a groundswell of support from the staff.

Most secondary school schedule builders inherit a schedule from their predecessors. These educators are charged with the daunting responsibility of piecing together a puzzle that will place students in classes of their choice with as little conflict as possible while also avoiding teacher and class conflicts and accommodating numerous individual classes, programs, and concerns. If the schedule deviates at all from what people (parents as well as teachers) have come to expect, the schedule builder is told that the schedule has been a certain way for years and that "it works." You should challenge that status quo. "It works" often means that it is efficient but not necessarily effective.

The best way we have found to approach major schedule adjustments at the secondary level is to rebuild the master schedule from the beginning. Most schedule software programs will allow a second master schedule to be built without deleting the current master schedule. These software programs are not required to develop a working draft, however. Some schedule builders draft a master with paper and pencil by listing each department on a separate sheet of paper with running tallies (hand-calculated course and section enrollment numbers) at the bottom of each sheet to ensure balance from one period to the other. We prefer to use a spreadsheet and insert calculation formulas for subsections of the master schedule.

As you start this process, keep in mind that the primary reason for restructuring the schedule is to increase student achievement through teacher collaboration—not to accommodate special requests from teachers. We do like to tell teachers as far in advance as possible what they will be teaching the following year, but we do not support guaranteeing them specific hours of the day for certain classes or planning periods. A good rule of thumb is to schedule students first and then teachers, and to be transparent about the changes to the master schedule. If you can accommodate teacher preferences after scheduling the students, great. And, of course, there may be extenuating circumstances, such as a half-time teacher whose classes must obviously be scheduled when he or she is in the building.

When we have initiated major schedule changes, the first courses we placed in the master to provide appropriate supervision and coverage were the physical education classes. You might ask, "What does that have to do with academic improvement?" Well, maybe not much. But if you don't have adequate coverage in the locker rooms and schedule the boys' and girls' classes respectfully with the physical education teachers, you may find yourself needing to ask others in the building to help with locker room coverage at the beginning and end of each period.

Expect to face some pushback from staff if scheduling common time for collaboration is new to your school.

The next periods to be scheduled in the master should be the ones you have chosen as common planning periods for specific departments. Those periods should be held sacred; you must commit to not scheduling any classes covering that subject during the dedicated common time. Some schedule builders will tell you that this is not possible and instead plan common time by specific course or grade level. We do not recommend this approach because some teachers teach more than one course or grade level within a department (e.g., English 9, English 10, and English 12). If you scheduled the common time by course or grade level, it would be impossible to provide these teachers with periods during the day to collaborate with colleagues who teach the same courses.

It is important to maintain balance for each period of the day. If there are 900 students in the building, there must be at least 900 available seats for instruction during each period. We have experienced a few cases in which we were not able to give all students all the courses they requested, but this issue existed under the old schedule as well. Under the new schedule, the same number of teachers will be off during a given period; the only difference is that those periods are determined according to their teaching responsibilities (see Resource 15).

Scheduling common time works a little differently for elementary schools. Unlike middle and high schools, most elementary schools do not have dedicated periods of the day, but you can still create time for collaboration. For example, you could schedule an activity for students led by teachers who don't teach English and have the teachers who do teach English focus on the English curriculum during that time. You can also schedule common time during students' special periods, which traditionally include physical education, art, music, and other classes that do not require the presence of their grade-level teachers.

We also recommend initiating a homeroom period in elementary schools in addition to high schools. When creating the homeroom sections, be sure to build enough slack into the schedule to keep a number of positions (including teachers, instructional assistants, secretaries, librarians, aides, and administrators) free of classroom responsibilities during that time. You can do this by increasing the homeroom class sizes to ensure that all teachers who should be clued in on meetings about specific curricula are able to be. Then rotate the homeroom assignments to allow all teachers their opportunity to collaborate on content. We suggest using this homeroom time to support such school initiatives as reading, math, citizenship skills, character skills, career awareness, or life or study skills. Do not use this time for study hall, however; that would be as good as saying, "My school has nothing more to offer your children during the instructional day, so they can do anything they want during this period as long as they are quiet and comply with the rules." This is not how schools achieve academic excellence.

Building common collaboration time into the day benefits administrators as well as students and teachers. Because of their numerous job demands, many administrators are not as involved with their teams or departments as they might like to be. They often have difficulty attending before- and after-school team or department meetings because those times tend to conflict with all the professional responsibilities that consume their time: meeting with parents, placing substitutes, addressing issues that have arisen on the bus run, monitoring students' departure in the afternoon, covering extracurricular and athletic activities, returning phone calls and e-mails, and so on.

So the shift toward common time during the school day enables administrators to increase their involvement and monitor what actually goes on in teams and departments. They can attend meetings with much less conflict to their own schedules. Attending regular, embedded meetings rather than isolated, monthly meetings outside of contract hours helps them forge learning partnerships and promote professional growth by participating in instructional dialogues. Such involvement shows administrators as partners rather than as overt supervisors, active participants in change rather than bystanders directing change.

Find More Minutes

Another way to find more time is to reconsider how your school allocates time. One area from which you can shave minutes is the passing time between class periods. Reducing passing time could give teachers more time to work with one another during the school day.

We have been in a number of schools that reduced the time between classes for this purpose. A large Maryland high school with a seven-period day reduced its 10-minute passing time to 5 minutes. Both students and staff may perceive this as a major change that affects the school culture. So teachers will need to be on board, helping to usher students to class and supporting the new passing time among both students and their colleagues. In a school with seven periods, this change allows for 30 "extra" minutes each day during which students can engage in constructive activities while teachers meet to discuss curriculum and professional practice. This option does require some thought with regard to class coverage and room locations, but it's a viable choice. For example, this time could serve as a student activity period (e.g., chess club, yearbook, technology team, and so on) supervised by teachers who are not involved in the collaboration for that day.

You might also ask your shared leadership team members to find extra time during the day or week; empower them to be creative, then listen to what they say. For example, they might propose using substitutes already in the building to give teachers an extra free period or allowing teachers to cover classes outside their own discipline to allow teams to meet. Finally, consider asking your math lead teacher to help calculate minutes to find "hidden" time.

To get more ideas on ways to adjust the schedule, ask other educators how their schedule is structured.

Plan Delayed Openings

Delayed openings are generally associated with inclement weather. But imagine what could be accomplished if a school incorporated some extra delayed openings into its calendar year. The school or district would still get credit for the day, and teachers would be able to collaborate with one another for as long as two hours during the contract day. This is a practical and cost-effective option because you won't need to pay teachers to stay after the contract day has ended, and you don't have to worry about finding coverage for classes to enable teachers to meet. Another idea is to scatter some early dismissals throughout the school year. Many elementary schools already do this, so why not try it at the high school level?

As long as parents are notified about these changes in advance, these are viable options that have only a minor impact on the school day. It is important that you clearly communicate the reason for these calendar changes to offset any feelings of frustration or resentment from parents who are inconvenienced by them. You might mention early dismissals and delayed openings in your school improvement plan, which you can post on your school's Web site, so that parents under-

Be sure to set the tone on delayed openings and early dismissal days so that staff know you're serious and committed to the concept of working together, not to the idea of socializing.

stand the rationale and expectation behind this change. You could also publish these dates in the school newsletter, post them on the marquee, and phone a call-out as a reminder as the date nears. If you explain that these days are structured times to help teachers grow as professionals so that they can better serve their students, most parents will accept the decision.

Eliminate Meetings

If you are a principal and want to give your teachers time during the contract day to work together, don't forget to look in your own backyard. In one midwestern high school that was on a state watch list for failing to meet its AYP benchmarks, administrators suspected that if they could give their teachers more time to collaborate on curriculum, instruction, and data, they might improve academic achievement and get off the watch list. They held several discussions on how to make that happen without spending money and decided to reduce the number of monthly faculty meetings, instead structuring that time for teachers to collaborate.

Administrators also agreed that when faculty members did have to meet, they would eliminate informational items from the agenda and use the time in a more productive, professional manner. As Jim Collins (2001) observes, people who have built effective companies make "as much use of 'stop doing' lists as 'to do' lists" and display "a remarkable discipline to unplug all sorts of extraneous junk" (p. 139). This administration believed that too many faculty meetings contained "extraneous junk" in the form of informational items and announcements. During the revised faculty meetings, information was shared at the very beginning, and it was limited to essential items. After these brief announcements, teachers broke into groups according to their disciplines and concentrated either on data and particular team needs or on a focus question provided by the administrators. Time reserved for faculty meetings became time to work with and learn from colleagues. This change meant a lot to the staff because by changing the status quo to better accommodate the school's current educational demands, the principal was modeling behavior that he expected from the teachers.

Transform District or Centralized Inservice Days

Many districts hold mandatory inservice days during the summer when school-based staff members travel to a central location for training or an informational meeting. But what if schools were allowed to hold their own site-based staff development days in the summer? This model would still allow for the announcement of county initiatives, curriculum updates, and other centralized information. If the district requires specific training from the central office, a representative from each curriculum or grade-level team could attend the centrally provided training and then conduct turnaround training during the site-based inservice day. The remaining time in the day could be used for specific site-based training and teacher collaboration.

Think how often teachers come back from districtwide inservices complaining that they didn't do anything relevant or that their days were a waste of time. Consider those teachers who observe that those mandatory training days prevent them from doing truly important work, such as looking at data and adjusting their delivery of the curriculum. There would need to be some administrative oversight with scheduling and managing these inservice opportunities, but this model enables schools to address their own particular needs in a collaborative manner—something especially important in larger districts whose schools have different populations and concerns.

Some central office staff may struggle with this concept. If this is the case in your school system, you may need to discuss your plans well in advance of next year's summer inservices. Be sure to identify the specific outcomes—including academic data and culminating products—that you expect to result from developing and delivering your own inservice days. Overall, this idea should appeal to central office staff members, especially when they consider how much money the school system can save by avoiding such expenses as mileage reimbursement and renting out conference locations. They may recognize and appreciate that you are not just attempting to satisfy individual school needs but also trying to save the district money and time.

Reconsider Working Lunches

The idea of working lunches always comes up during discussions of finding additional professional time because it is usually easy to schedule teachers of a given subject area to have the same lunch period. Some administrators try to make this an attractive option with catchy names like "Lunch and Learn" or "Potluck and Pedagogy." However, we believe that lunchtime should be sacrosanct. Everyone should be entitled to unencumbered time to eat, decompress, and recharge before facing the second half of the school day.

If working lunches *are* floated as an option, the idea needs to come from the staff on a voluntary basis and then be supported by the shared leadership team. We have been in many schools where teachers used their lunch breaks to remediate students, collaborate on curriculum, and develop common assessments. We found that some teachers embraced working lunches because they saw them as a better alternative to staying after school; however, many teachers soon lost their enthusiasm for professional conversations because they started to resent this intrusion on "their time." And when working lunches are a directive, you will likely be responding to reduced morale and working out complaints and grievances with district-level leadership and union or association representatives. If it is the teachers' idea, be sure to document the request; if it is your idea, leave it alone. It is always best when extended work time arises from desire, not directives.

Address Resistance

It is a common refrain that we hear over and over again: how do you handle resistance? Not everyone will like the idea of collaborating with their colleagues, so how do you get everyone engaged and working with the same level of effort and motivation?

There is no magic pill that will make staff members do what you ask of them. What you can and should do is deal with resistance in a direct fashion, early on. When you do, you need to connect your conversation to the norms and expectations that you have already established and note the disconnect that you observe between the expectations and the actions of the resistant teacher. When you address one resister early on, you could well be addressing several staff members unbeknownst to you: now everyone knows that this is behavior you won't tolerate. With that initial conversation, you also begin the documentation trail in case the behavior does not change.

In one midwestern school with a population of nearly 1,700 students, the principal decided to implement common planning time for teachers. He explained how teacher collaboration would benefit teachers and students alike, and in small groups, the message seemed to go down well, with most teachers being willing to adopt the new idea and agreeing that it was good for the school. However, at the larger faculty meeting we conducted, one teacher interrupted the meeting in an unprofessional manner by exclaiming, "I have had enough of this! I am so busy and frustrated that I can't even think about doing something different!"

We asked her to describe specifically what she meant by "frustrated." After a few minutes, it became clear that she had several frustrations and was not going to be receptive to possible solutions. Her issues could not be resolved in this setting. If you find yourself in a similar position, whether as a teacher leader in a small-group meeting or as an administrator at a large-group meeting, we recommend choosing one of the two following responses:

- I appreciate your openness and candor, but as you can see from the agenda, we are getting off track. I see that others are ready to move forward, so I will make time later to discuss this in more detail. Are you able to move forward with us now?

- If I am reading this correctly, you are upset, and I don't want to be the catalyst to this situation. If you don't feel you can sit here any longer, I don't mind if you excuse yourself from the meeting. We can discuss this matter further in the near future.

However, for right now I don't want this issue to monopolize the meeting any longer, so I need to move forward on the agenda.

Handling this kind of situation in a professional and nonconfrontational manner will prevent you from losing support from the rest of the staff. There is no reason to make a person feel embarrassed or ashamed in front of his or her peers. However, in a one-on-one discussion, this teacher does need to hear clearly that his or her unprofessional behavior is not acceptable. This conversation is especially important coming from an administrator because

- The teacher hears a clear message that the behavior is not acceptable. (Expectations are outlined.)
- It will filter out to other staff in the building. (Expectations are reinforced and spread.)
- Other teachers will appreciate knowing that the behavior was addressed. (Effective teachers want accountability.)
- It provides preliminary documentation if the behavior persists. (Your personal record, which should include the date, the time, and a brief outline of the discussion, will help you in case you need to recall the situation in the future.)

When you need to document behavior, simply state during the conversation that you will follow up in writing to ensure that both parties have a record of fact. Doing so helps to avoid future surprises.

In most cases, you should not put the first occurrence in writing or in the recalcitrant teacher's local file—everybody is entitled to a bad day—but you do need to be straightforward during the conversation and explain that continued outbursts of this nature may result in formal documentation (e.g., a letter in the local personnel file). This sets the stage in case you have to revisit the issue with the teacher and need formal documentation to begin professional development efforts. If the teacher doesn't respond favorably, this documentation will help you begin the removal process. The situation is bound to cause ripples throughout the school, which is not a bad thing. Sometimes you need to remind staff members that they must consistently demonstrate professional behavior when they work with such a precious commodity: children.

Don't Waste Time, Find More of It

We cannot stress it enough: time is a premium. Therefore, we encourage you not to waste any of it by conducting needs assessments to determine whether your teachers need more of it. You already know that if you need it, then they need it, too. Some administrators distribute tracking tools that have teachers record how they spend their free periods to show how they could benefit from collaborating with their colleagues. We believe that this task is counterproductive, taking time away from more important work and further fomenting feelings of alienation and frustration among teachers. When we are in schools that use time tracking, teachers tend to believe that the "powers that be" truly do not understand or remember what goes on in the trenches—because if they did, surely they would not require teachers to use precious time in such a manner!

The responsibilities that go along with being educators cannot be discharged within seven and a half hours; we are kidding ourselves if we think they can. Today, teachers are being asked to do more than ever. It's not necessary to spend more time to learn this. Far more useful is to find ways to give you and your staff more time. But creating professional time only solves half of the problem; the next step is ensuring that the time is used as productively as possible.

Getting Started

- Reflect on what you do during your day and how you might be able to maximize your time.
- Research and review how other schools have structured their days.
- Build in common collaboration time for staff members.
- Brainstorm creative, innovative ways to manipulate your time and schedule.

6

Facilitating Effective Meetings

Just because staff members have the time to meet doesn't mean that the time they spend together will be productive—a simultaneously disheartening and frightening thought! Many of us educators are social creatures by nature, so when we are given time with colleagues, we embrace it as a time to socialize. But after investing so much effort into finding time to facilitate teacher collaboration, your meetings should not be used as "talk time." Nor should meetings consist of announcements that could have been made through e-mail. Teachers sleepwalk through these kinds of meetings as passive participants—much as some of our less engaged students do in class!

In healthy cultures, meetings are a time for powerful, active professional development and dialogue. Attendees are discussing instruction, creating assessments, analyzing data, and discussing students—not listening to colleagues or supervisors read aloud informational items. The potential of teachers actively engaged and working toward their own growth with the help and support of colleagues should not be underestimated. To make the most of this potential, you need to safeguard against time thievery at meetings and help your teachers learn how to work together.

Implement Parameters, Practices, and Procedures

Agreed-upon processes and clear expectations are the best means to maximize a team's efficacy and minimize time thievery during meetings. Squandered meetings are a curious but not uncommon feature of schools, despite being filled with highly skilled and educated professionals. So staff members often need to be taught how to get the most out of their meetings. As the oft-quoted football coach Vince Lombardi once commented, "The question is usually not how well each person works, but how well they work together." An important way to avoid the common pitfalls of meetings, then, is to transform the reason and the way we meet.

Have a Purpose

When we discuss educators meeting—whether as a team, a department, or a committee—we are again referring to "a group of people with complementary skills who are committed to a common purpose, performance goals, and common approach for which they hold themselves mutually accountable" (Katzenbach & Smith, 1993, p. 111). One of the key words in that description is *purpose*. We have attended too many meetings that lack purpose and therefore lack interest, enthusiasm, and momentum. If the meeting has no purpose, why should anyone come?

Facilitate and guide discussions and outcomes by asking open-ended questions.

If you are new to a school and haven't inherited meeting processes and procedures, you may find that attendees discuss random subjects at meetings. If this is the case, don't try to break the trend immediately and autocratically, or you run the risk of alienating your new colleagues. First, take time to observe the meetings and the way they function while contributing as an active participant. After you have formed some perceptions, you can express your need to better understand the purpose of the meetings and the responsibilities of attendees. Bringing up these issues can bring to light the lack of meeting structures and offer an opportunity to discuss purpose. You might start by asking, "You know, during the last couple of meetings I have wondered about something; could you help me understand . . . ?" or "Could you help me out by explaining . . . ?" It is easier to find out about processes by asking open-ended questions than by passing judgment. A well-posed question invites others to participate and is therefore a less threatening way of directing the necessary outcome.

On the other hand, observations or questions like "I don't think we have a common understanding of the purpose of our meetings" and "Do you understand why we meet, other than because we have to?" are really judgments in disguise, too abrupt to open up a productive dialogue and apt to put the recipient on the defensive. They will likely offend your colleagues and erode trust, resulting in even more difficulty in trying to bring about change. Understanding how to better pose questions or present information is an important part of helping any school and its staff thrive.

One school we worked in had numerous teams that held regular meetings. For the purpose of this scenario, we will highlight only a few of the major ones:

- The Administrative Team met weekly and included the principal, the assistant principals, the School Resource Officer, and the principal's administrative assistant.

- The Instructional Council met weekly and included the principal, the assistant principals, the department chairs, and the Interdisciplinary Team leaders.

- The Faculty Advisory Committee met monthly and included the principal and five to seven members who were voted onto the committee by the faculty.

- The Interdisciplinary Team met two to three times a week and included all teachers on the team and any grade-level elective teachers who did not have classroom responsibilities during the meeting time.

These different teams' meetings often covered the same subjects, and several of the staff members who served on more than one committee or team were aware of this. This overlap in meeting topics led us to inquire what the purpose of these meetings was and demonstrated to us that the team members were not sure, either.

Not all meetings are a senseless waste of time, of course. However, unless each meeting has a different purpose and agenda, it will become known as just another meeting that staff members attend because they have to. These kinds of situations erode morale and hinder productivity. With a few special exceptions (e.g., meetings dealing with safety and security or celebrations for staff members' personal milestones), every meeting's general purpose should fall under one of the following categories:

- Academic achievement;
- School improvement; or
- Staff development.

There is some overlap among these areas, but the structures and rules that we recommend and that your teams adopt will help keep meetings focused. If you are in doubt about the purpose of a meeting, ask yourself or the members of your team if the issue falls under one of the three core areas. If so, drill down deeper by asking *how* and *why* it does. If not, ask yourself and your team members whether the meeting deserves to occupy your time; if there are other more pressing issues, then you need to drop the item that is consuming discussion time. Finally, you should ask yourself if the meeting's main issue could have been easily addressed over e-mail rather than in a group setting.

Eliminating overlap between meetings through standardized agendas is another good way to maximize your time. While observing meetings, we found that although agenda formats and agenda items varied, the issues that came up and monopolized most of the meeting time were often the same from one meeting to the next. Issues that surfaced again and again included student behavior in the cafeteria, staff morale, staff restrooms, student restrooms, vending machines, photocopiers, hallway conduct, tardy policies, absence policies, insufficient parent support, excessive parent support, lack of student interest, and the number of required meetings. We appreciated the irony in the last issue.

We met with each group in the school to clarify and document the purpose of its meetings and to decide how it would like to conduct its meetings. Most team members did not share a common understanding of the purpose of their meetings. In a workshop with the school's staff, we found that everyone was able to verbalize his or her version of the purpose, but there was little evidence that the meetings satisfied the multitude of purposes.

The expenditure of human resources on these kinds of unfocused meetings is mind-boggling. Bringing a more sharpened focus to these groups streamlines the bureaucracy and increases the effectiveness of teachers, teams, departments, and the school as a whole. As a bonus, increasing efficacy in this way actually saves money.

One productive exercise to help a team or department identify its common purpose has each member share his or her perception of the purpose first. Begin by distributing copies of the table in Resource 16. Then ask each member of the team to draft his or her interpretation of the team's purpose in the first row of the table; for this portion of the activity, there should be no discussion or sharing of opinions. After team members have finished their personal drafts, divide the team into groups of five. Have each group sit at a round table. Each member then has one minute to tell the other four group members how he or she defines the team's purpose.

During this time, the rest of the group listens without interruption and takes notes in the additional rows of the table. After the first group member has finished sharing his or her purpose statement, the group takes one minute for questions and clarification. The group repeats this process of sharing and questioning until every member has shared his or her identified purpose.

During the next stage, each small group takes 10 minutes to draft a purpose that incorporates elements of the individual members' statements. When the groups have completed this task, they each designate a spokesperson to share the drafts with the entire team or department. If you are working with a larger group, such as an entire faculty, you should repeat the process from the previous paragraph after combining every two teams into one and allotting another 10 minutes for the combined teams to draft a purpose. Continue this process until a single purpose can be agreed on. Then write down the date on which the statement was created as well as a date to revisit and revise the statement, if necessary. Our recommendation is not to allow this date to exceed a six-month time frame.

Once the team adopts a purpose, it can then use it as a guide to determine the appropriateness of team business. Teams could even include the purpose on the agenda for every meeting to keep it at the forefront of people's minds. In the school we worked with, faculty members increased the productivity of their meetings by keeping discussions focused on the teams' purpose. For example, the Faculty Advisory Committee agreed that any items from the faculty involving instructional decisions would be submitted to the Instructional Council for its agenda. When items came up in Instructional Council meetings that had to do with school functions or processes, they were submitted to the Faculty Advisory Committee for resolution. The Administrative Team was able to stay focused on administrative issues and developed the ability to quickly identify items that needed to be distributed to other teams for resolution or for recommendations.

Establish Norms

Norms are standards, or what is expected from team members and meetings. Without well-developed and documented norms, meetings can be chaotic and unfocused, resulting in frustration and a lack of team commitment. Here are some basic norms that were collectively developed by the aforementioned Instructional Council:

- All meetings will have an agenda.
- All items discussed in the meeting will relate to instruction, not facilities or behavior.
- All members are expected to participate in meaningful discussion.
- Note-taking responsibility will rotate through the meeting membership.
- Notes will be recorded from each meeting and distributed to the members and posted for staff.
- All members are expected to attend each meeting.
- When a member will be absent, he or she will inform his or her supervisor in advance and send a substitute to the meeting.
- Disagreements will be discussed during the meeting and not outside the meeting.
- When the team makes decisions and total consensus does not seem possible, the team will openly discuss all points of view and develop total commitment to support the decision.
- Members must not bring unrelated work to the meeting.
- Meetings will start and end on time.
- Meetings will be held solely for discussion and decision making; one-way communication will be limited or eliminated whenever possible by sending e-mail or memorandums in advance.
- Everyone owns the meeting.

- When items surface that are not on the agenda, the team will decide to adjust the current agenda or add the items to the next agenda.
- The team will vote on a meeting facilitator for the year and identify backup facilitators to run meetings in the facilitator's absence.

These standards enabled the Instructional Council to be more productive because they provided structure and let all members know what was expected of them. We welcome you to use these norms or some version of them for your own meetings (see Resource 17). In addition to these, your team may want to consider such norms as announcing meeting dates in advance; practicing confidentiality; reading the previous meeting's minutes before the next meeting; and avoiding side conversations and other disrespectful behavior during meetings. A helpful process we have used in developing norms is asking team members to identify specific aspects of meetings that they like and aspects that they dislike; such a discussion enables them to come to a shared agreement on what could be called their norms.

Set a goal of developing the first draft of your team's norms in 30 minutes. Then continue to review the norms at each meeting until they are lived by all members.

Before the Instructional Council developed its meeting guidelines, the Administrative Team went through the same process of developing its own norms. This gave administrators the experience and skills necessary to help the rest of the staff make the transition to meeting norms. After the Instructional Council developed and adopted its agenda format, each member took the same strategy to his or her department to implement a similar process.

Use Agendas

Some leaders balk at the idea of having agendas for meetings. We realize how strange that might sound, but we have known leaders who believe that agendas are too rigid and prefer what they believe could be a freer exchange of ideas. The point these leaders are missing is that such idea swaps are most productive when they happen in a structured setting. For the most part, structure engenders productivity.

In addition to indicating what meetings will address, agendas should also include time guidelines for each item. Although it can be difficult to guess how much time to allot for each item, with experience you will discover that it is much like planning a lesson. Keeping that in mind, here are some questions to consider when creating your agendas:

- Are the agenda items connected to and prioritized in accordance with the vision, mission, or purpose of the team?
- What is the expected outcome of each agenda item?
- Have team members been solicited for agenda items?
- How long is the meeting?
- How many items are on the agenda?
- Are the agenda items new, or have they been previously discussed and understood?
- How long will it take for the group to discuss and conclude each item?
- How long do I realistically think the group can discuss a particular item before they start becoming disengaged?
- Should the item be sent out to team members in advance of the meeting?

You should consider these questions when identifying the appropriate amount of time to assign to the agenda items. If you allot 15 minutes to a particular item, the group will spend 15 minutes on that item. This is fine if 15 minutes are necessary, but if the group only needed 5 minutes, the meeting just wasted 10 minutes of professionals' time. Often, this extra time is filled with one or two attendees pontificating or parroting what each person before them has said.

If certain team members tend to monopolize meetings, the team should develop a norm to address the issue.

When nonagenda items surface during meetings, you should ensure that the discussion is brought back to the agenda, and any attendee can take the responsibility to call attention to the digression. Team members should not wait for someone else to bring the group back; everyone has a vested interest in time being used wisely. Refocusing conversations does not have to be done in a rude or unprofessional manner. It can be as easy as saying, "Excuse me, I must have lost track somewhere during the discussion and don't see where this issue is listed on the agenda; did I miss something?" or "I'm sorry, where are we on the agenda?"

The typical response is something along the lines of, "Oops—no, it was kind of a spin-off of what someone else said." In those cases, any of the meeting participants can easily redirect the conversation back to the agenda.

But there is another type of response that is more difficult to address: "You're right. It is not on the agenda, but this is very important and needs to be discussed." When someone makes this response, the meeting members need to collectively and promptly decide whether that item should be added to the agenda. If members agree to add it, they need to identify how much time to allot to it or decide whether to add it to the next meeting's agenda for a more prepared discussion. If the item is added to the current agenda, the team will have to make time adjustments for the remaining items.

Recently, we were in a staff development session discussing meeting structures and processes with a group of high school teachers. They commented that although they thought this type of structure made sense, they would like to be able to have some off-topic discussion time as well. They did not get to see one another outside these meetings, and their need for social interaction as a team was important to them. They believed that eliminating it would likely reduce their productivity. We told them that they didn't have to clone the structure we created and urged them to use our suggestions as a foundation to build on. Each circumstance is unique. In this case, we asked the participants to brainstorm what they felt would work while keeping the structure they liked. After a short discussion, the team decided to include a running five-minute agenda item dedicated to informal discussion.

At first, they allotted the first five minutes of the meeting to this informal discussion. After several meetings, however, the team found that it had difficulty adhering to the agenda after establishing a casual tone. In addition, some team members had no interest in informal discussions and even started arriving late, thinking they knew when the real business of the meeting would start. The team revisited its decision and decided to move the unstructured time to the end of the agenda, allowing members to leave before or during that time.

Conclude meetings and discussions with next–step action plans for what should take place before the next collaboration time.

A final point regarding agendas is that you should generally distribute them to team members at least a couple of days before the meeting. If you wish to have members participate in a meaningful manner, you should enable them to ponder the agenda items in advance (see Resource 18).

Keep a Record

Have you ever left a meeting confident that everyone was on the same page, heard the same things you did, and reached the same conclusions you did, only to be stupefied later when everyone had a slightly different recollection? This is the reason why many effective schools have decided that if a meeting is important enough to occur regularly and have an agenda, it is important enough to take notes for.

These notes or minutes are your team's collective memory. Their purpose is to capture key discussions, outcomes, and actions from one meeting to the next. After the meeting, members can take an opportunity to review and revise the minutes if necessary. Keeping this kind of record helps avoid confusion and conflict over what was meant and what was remembered. The notes then serve as a professional contract for the team.

Some teachers feel anxious at the prospect of taking minutes because they think they must provide a word-for-word record of meetings. However, the notes we recommend are not meant to be labor-intensive; they can be short and sweet and still describe the important aspects of a meeting. To make it easier, the note taker can enter notes directly into an electronic version of the meeting agenda. If you choose to use the agenda format in Resource 18, the note taker could just add another line to the table below the agenda item being discussed. This way, the note taker would have the majority of the notes complete at the meeting's adjournment.

Invite Participation

Team members' full participation is required for meaningful meetings. We are not talking about absorbing information announced by a select few members, silently agreeing or disagreeing with it, and then departing. That is attendance, not participation. You might ask your teachers to consider and discuss the following question: "Do all of us really want this meeting to be run and owned by a few vocal members?" If the group's answer is no, then everyone must commit to active participation. If the answer is a shrug and a nod of acceptance, then team members should ask themselves, "If we don't mind a couple of the members guiding the group and making the decisions, then why should the rest of us attend the meetings?" Certainly most could find better things to do with their time than wait in a room for a couple of people to make decisions for them.

So members need to decide whether they want to be contributing meeting members or passive recipients of meeting outcomes.

Some members will ask themselves, "Is something going to happen in this meeting that will change my responsibilities, my life, my world?" Only when the outcome of a meeting has personal-professional changing potential do members tend to get more involved and more attentive to the details of the items discussed. If team members do not predict a meaningful outcome, they should ask, "Why are we discussing this item?" and "Why are we attending this meeting?"

Meeting participants can make the leap from identifying participation expectations to acting on them in several ways. When first implementing some of these strategies, they might feel awkward or uncomfortable. But with practice, the behaviors will become a normal, natural part of the meetings. The meeting structure should allow each member to respond to discussion items and contribute to each decision. Any team member should be able to say, "Emily, Tom, have you weighed in on this topic, or did I miss your contribution?" If the team follows the norm that requires all members to participate in meaningful discussion, then Emily and Tom should have something to contribute or an opinion on the direction of the discussion.

You can encourage participation by implementing a round-robin strategy until discussions flow more naturally. Bring up a proposed solution or decision and have all the team members around the table state in turn whether the decision is something they can support. If they cannot support it, then they need to explain why and recommend adjustments to the decision. If they agree with the decision, they should offer a specific example of how they will support or defend it. Each time someone suggests a revision to the decision or solution, the round-robin begins again with that person first.

Another example of a situation that would warrant full participation is the introduction of nonagenda items. The whole team needs to decide whether to adjust the current agenda to include the item or postpone the discussion until the next meeting. Although this takes time from the current meeting, it is more efficient than addressing each item as it arises. Postponing the items until the next meeting provides members with time to reflect, gather data, and generally prepare to fully engage in meaningful conversation. What you might discover, though, is that by February you have so many unresolved agenda items that they need an entire meeting of their own! In one high school in Montgomery County, Maryland, the Administrative Team found itself running into this problem. Items kept surfacing that detracted from the current agenda, overwhelming team members and consuming valuable time. Eventually, the team devised a summertime "parking lot list," or a list of items that were not yet ready to be brought into the building for discussion and so were left in the "parking lot" until there was time for them—generally the summer.

Establish Meeting Roles

Another way to invite full participation is to establish meeting roles. Consider rotating these responsibilities to ensure that all team members get to be equal contributors to and owners of the meetings. Rotating roles also helps avoid having to cancel meetings when one person is absent. Some schools rotate responsibilities as a way of cross-training different leadership positions. Other schools like having fixed roles to give meetings a level of consistency. If you opt for fixed roles, then build leadership capacity among the current team membership by having one or two backups for each position to maintain continuity.

Team Leader/Chair. Aside from being the liaison to supervisors or administrators, the team leader is the person who sets the agenda. He or she reminds members about the meeting and distributes the agenda and any pertinent materials like handouts or articles prior to the meeting. The team leader sets the tone of the meeting by reviewing the agenda items or giving an overview of the purpose at the beginning of the meeting. He or she might also inquire whether anyone has a last-minute addition to the agenda or needs time at the end of the meeting to make announcements. During the meeting, he or she actively encourages all members to participate.

Facilitator/Timekeeper. Many teams combine these two roles, but some separate them to actively involve more people in the meetings. The facilitator/timekeeper is responsible for guiding the flow of discussion and monitoring the pacing of the meeting. He or she ensures that one or two people do not dominate the meeting by soliciting input from other members and informs the chair when the allotted time for a topic is about to expire. Overall, the facilitator/timekeeper makes sure that the team adheres to timelines and directs the verbal traffic of meetings, ensuring that there are no snarls or jams along the way.

Recorder. More than the other meeting roles, the note-taking responsibility is a good one to rotate. Rotating the role prevents every meeting record from coming from a single point of view and ensures that there are backup recorders if the current one is absent. The recorder records the important points of the meeting, using the agenda as a guide. He or she distributes meeting notes after the meeting in a timely fashion, preferably within a day or two, while the content is still fresh in team members' minds. He or she solicits feedback and corrections regarding the minutes and then sends out a final version.

Understand Group Dynamics

Even with norms and structures in place, working effectively with different personality types and defusing tense situations take time and practice. It is helpful to understand the dynamics that occur in a team setting. Specifically, understanding the changes that occur as a team begins to come into its own will save you time and energy. In this section, we draw on Bruce Tuckman's (1965) model, which explains the necessary and inevitable stages a team goes through on the path toward efficacy.

Forming

Do you remember the song in *The King and I* that goes, "Getting to know you, getting to know all about you/Getting to like you, getting to hope you like me"? Well, that pretty much sums up what happens during this first stage. In this period of your team's infancy, members are forming impressions and relationships. As a general rule of thumb, people want to be liked and accepted, so team members are generally amicable and polite and avoid stepping on one another's toes. They maintain personally safe distances, offering little important personal information. During this stage, people are also gathering information about the leadership; even if team members are wary of the leadership or of working on a team, they will generally "allow" the team leader to lead while they assess his or her abilities.

What Forming Means for You. In this early stage, some staff members will be excited to be a part of a team, while others will be suspicious, cynical, or pessimistic. You should not be disappointed if the team seems to be taking longer than anticipated to complete tasks; this is natural. This stage has more to do with forming group practices and processes than actually achieving goals. Don't be distracted by members who are impatient with all the discussion about team behavior; these dialogues are a necessary component of transforming the group into a high-functioning team in the future. This is also an opportune time to develop the team's purpose or mission and expectations. To get the most out of your team during this stage, you need to facilitate this process of relationship building through team and trust activities.

Storming

As the slogan for MTV's seminal reality show *The Real World* goes, "Find out what happens when people stop being polite and start getting real." Quite simply, the honeymoon has ended at the storming stage, a period mainly marked by conflict and confrontation. Tensions build, and people start getting on one another's nerves;

professional disagreements amplify annoyances from minor idiosyncrasies. As people's true colors are shown, members try to convert others to their viewpoint to establish their own leadership. Those who were always opposed to working as a team take advantage of this period to more vocally express their doubts and dissatisfaction. All of these storms prevent headway, as conflicts cloud the team's purpose and progress toward its goals.

What Storming Means for You. These storms are a healthy and necessary part of growing as a team; there is no growth without struggle. Patience here is a virtue. The best thing you can do during this stage is acknowledge what the team is going through and help members understand the stages of team development. Too many leaders ignore this stage, fearing that it reflects poorly on them both

Just because a team has gone through the storming stage does not mean that it can't slip back into it.

personally and professionally. Unfortunately, ignoring dissent leads to more frustration and discord. During this stage, you will also notice the formation of opposing factions and cliques. We use each of these words purposefully because some storms will relate to people's professional viewpoints, while others will relate to their social relationships. Openly and honestly addressing conflicts by relying on established structures and processes can help bring the team back to the right track. That process may entail lending an ear for people to vent to or even a shoulder to cry on. In other cases, individual meetings and conferences will be necessary to move the team forward.

Norming

As the team resolves its conflicts and strengthens support for the previously established purpose and processes, it is well on its way toward becoming an effective, productive collective (see Resource 17). The group dynamics have stabilized, and people for the most part have accepted the team concept. During this stage, how the team functions becomes the norm, or the standard.

What Norming Means for You. Although excitement might have ebbed in the last stage, the team is now enthusiastically working as a more cohesive unit. Your responsibility is to nurture that enthusiasm. Encourage people to take risks and celebrate the gains the team has made. Some members begin to bond; others might still not accept all their fellow team members, but they do tolerate one another. Sometimes tolerance is the best you can hope for.

Performing

In this final stage, "people realize that they can achieve cooperative goals when day-to-day organizational norms of reciprocity encourage them to share information, listen to each other's ideas, exchange resources, and respond to each other's requests through positive interdependence . . . people will collaborate when they can actively contribute to the goal of making a whole from their separate pieces" (Kouzes & Posner, 2002, p. 282). The team has finally clicked and functions as a well-oiled machine. It focuses on shared goals and vision and performs equally well with or without the presence and guidance of the team leader. The team frequently surpasses identified goals and demonstrates a high degree of autonomy with a low level of supervision. Members hold themselves and one another accountable while providing support with difficult tasks and new projects. The team embraces disagreements as opportunities to hear different perspectives. Team norms are transparent and have become second nature.

What Performing Means for You. As well as the team is performing, it is possible for it to revert to a previous stage because of an especially challenging task or the addition of a new team member, so you should try to anticipate what the next storm on the horizon might be and when it will arrive.

Know Your Team Members

No matter how structured your meetings are, how well accepted your norms are, and how well you understand the changes your team will undergo, you are ultimately dealing with people—people who have the potential to jeopardize the team's focus. Your challenge is to handle these team members to maintain your team's productivity. Below we offer examples of some of the more common personality types on teams and advice on how to work with them.

The Know-It-All

Every team has one: the person who has seen it all and done it all. This person will top anything you say. He is often the first to explain that something won't work because it was tried five years ago and failed. He is eager to share stories that support his claim and that often derail the meeting and create new topics for gossip. Working with him can be tough because while you want to recognize his knowledge and institutional history, your goal is to move toward change. You also need to move ahead with the meeting agenda.

The best way to work with him is to ask him during the meeting why the proposed idea failed before. Not only does this validate his sense of history, but it can also give you some much-needed background information. If he responds with something vague like, "It was a disaster," ask for specific facts. In other large-group situations, you might respond with something like, "Stan, I hear what you have to say about this; would you be willing to hear what Susan has to say? She could have something to offer here." Once you have identified the know-it-all, you can also conserve the team's time by approaching him outside of meetings. He desires an audience, and it's powerful to have a personal audience with the team's leader.

The Skeptic

The skeptic might also believe that she knows it all, but she is more likely to spend time doubting and questioning whatever is on the table, whether or not she possesses the institutional history that the know-it-all does. Her colleagues are likely to view her as the negative force on the team. You don't need to devote time to her outside of meetings, but the skeptic is actually someone you want on your side. Because she is quick to air her doubts and tell you why things won't work, you can learn to rely on her to show you potential pitfalls and shortcomings in your proposal.

Team members often look your way for nonverbal cues. Be aware of your own facial, body, and other nonverbal communications. Hide them when necessary, but also learn how to use them with intent.

The Disagreer

The aspect that distinguishes the disagreer from the know-it-all and the skeptic is that the disagreer is usually quite noticeable in his disagreement with you. He may shake his head or snort loudly to express his displeasure or even openly challenge you. Sometimes the disagreer is a bully at heart, sometimes a know-it-all in disguise. The best way to disarm him is to call him on his actions. When you see him vigorously shaking his head at the next meeting, simply say, "Tom, I see you shaking your head; it seems that you disagree with what is being said. Could you share why?" In most cases, this ends the discussion because he is embarrassed by being called out. We don't recommend regularly taking this action, but when the disagreer's signs of dissent are obvious to all, you need to send a clear message in a professional manner.

The Overachiever

The overachiever is like that student who participates in numerous sports and extracurricular activities while managing to turn in consistently stellar work. She has already read that new article or tried that new idea and just seems to know so much. Many staff members—teachers and administrators alike—are threatened by this person, or at least don't know what to make of her. But the overachiever is definitely someone you want on your side; she might even end up being your biggest supporter. Encourage her, touch base with her, and tap into her knowledge base. Develop her leadership potential and validate her standing in the team by giving her tasks to accomplish. She needs attention, and the right type of attention will yield rich dividends.

The Underachiever

The underachiever does as little as possible. You can't regularly rely on him to complete tasks, but he will generally show up on time for meetings because he is committed to meeting minimum expectations and keeping that paycheck coming. In this case, you do not want to address his behavior publicly. Instead, you might ask him after the meeting if there is anything wrong or if there is anything he needs. Most likely, there isn't; he is probably just skating by and not doing anything flagrantly wrong. In this case, we recommend that you discuss the issue with your administrator if you are a teacher leader; if you are an administrator, we recommend that you lay out your expectations to the underachiever and start the process of documentation. The best way to preserve the team's time might be to avoid assigning tasks to him unless you think that he will complete them and not squander the team's time. You do need to address the behavior because otherwise you are signaling that it is acceptable, and you may end up creating a team of underachievers who drain your time and energy.

The Interrupter

In essence, the interrupter lacks respect for those who hold the floor (or she respects herself more!). She doesn't allow others to answer or finish what they are saying. Her behavior is not necessarily conscious or loaded with malicious intent, but it must be addressed so that she does not end up dominating meetings. You might say, "Thank you, Grace—now, Bill before you were interrupted you were saying _____; could you tell us the rest of your thoughts on that?" This approach should help the interrupter see her contributions as interruptions.

The Rambler

The rambler, like the know-it-all, eats up agenda time. Although he might start off with the best of intentions, he often goes off on a tangent and brings the rest of the team along for the ride. His topics might be school related, or they might be personal. A storyteller, he is not necessarily an unintelligent person; he is just someone who likes to talk. Your job will be pulling his energy back to the agenda items for decisions and closures.

The Parrot

The parrot is a cousin of the rambler in that she, too, is a talker. The difference is that she stays on topic. The problem is that she either paraphrases or repeats verbatim what has already been said. Don't confuse this as a show of support, although that is often her intention; it is more indicative of a deep-seated need to be recognized and validated. You can validate her, but that will just reinforce the behavior. Instead, you might want to establish a general ground rule asking people to comment only when they have new information to add.

The Rebel

The rebel is adversarial by nature. It does not matter who is in charge of what; he will oppose authority and push the envelope, just because. Some rebels are narcissists: they simply believe that they are better than everyone else. Even if there is not a case to rail against, the rebel believes he is earning some kind of credibility by doing so. So expect him to climb atop his soapbox to rant about what he perceives to be wrong and what he would do differently. The best way to handle him is to be direct and firm to prevent him from injecting toxicity into a meeting or steering the group away from its purpose. Use the agenda to bring him back to the meeting's focus.

The Late Arriver

If you announce a meeting for 2:30, she will arrive at 2:35. If you announce a meeting for 2:35, she will arrive at 2:40. No matter what time you schedule meetings, this person consistently arrives late to them, sending a negative message to others. The worst thing you can do is wait to start the meeting until this person arrives. By doing that, you are empowering her while conveying to team members that their time is not as important as hers. Treat your team with respect by respecting its time and beginning at agreed-upon times. Rather than openly addressing her tardiness in front of the team, discuss the issue with her individually. If the behavior continues, you may want to pursue documentation and note it in her evaluation.

The Early Leaver

Whether for a doctor's appointment, a trip to the car mechanic, or another meeting, this person always seems to leave meetings earlier than the designated end time. Sometimes he will give you his reason in advance; other times, he will announce it during the meeting or not say anything at all. This kind of behavior can be discouraging, and you may be tempted to end meetings when he leaves, believing that that's a better option than allowing the perceived floodgates of early leavers to open. But meetings shouldn't end because one person needs to leave early. A better way to handle the early leaver is to make it a norm at the beginning of the year to notify the facilitator or chair in advance of the need to leave early. If the early leaver continues his behavior on a regular basis, whether or not he notifies you in advance, you need to address him privately and possibly begin the documentation process.

Learning to Meet, Meeting to Learn

It's a reality that most teachers need to learn how to work in teams. It should actually come as no surprise, considering the fact that for decades the profession has trained teachers to work independently in individual classrooms. When thrust into collaborative situations, many teachers feel uncomfortable and defensive and hoard their knowledge. At worst, they are unable to function collectively because there are no structures in place to support them. But educators overall are intelligent and resilient professionals who desire to do well. So the norms and practices that we recommended in this chapter should ultimately be well received. Once these structures are in place, teachers can get down to the real business of analyzing data to improve their practice.

Getting Started

• Determine your team's purpose.

• Discuss with team members what makes teams and meetings effective or ineffective.

• As a team, create a list of norms and agreements that you will all abide by.

• Establish meeting roles for team members.

• Identify and share stages of team development with the team membership.

7

Mining and Using Data with Purpose

Our increased reliance on data is probably one of the greatest shifts to occur in the education field in more than a decade. We examine data to determine how things have been done in the past and to help us decide what to do next. Data allow for a level of measurement, analysis, and accountability that was, until relatively recently, nonexistent. In the 1990s, data in schools were usually synonymous with graduation rates and the number of students pursuing a postsecondary education; rarely were they used to drive instruction, decision making, and federal funding. Standardized testing and greater government involvement have irrevocably changed schools and the way they use data. It's more important than ever to learn how to get the most out of yours.

Identify Types of Data

There is no special secret to finding data in a school; they exist everywhere. The trick is to identify the types of data that you want your staff to be aware of and to determine how to use them.

Although we usually associate data with standardized test results, there are many different forms and types of data that influence academic achievement. Here we provide some examples of data that we have focused on in our work with schools. Many of these data could fit in one or more categories—for example, you could define teacher turnover statistics as administrative data *or* teacher data, and student grades could fall into the master schedule data category as well as the student data category. The categorization of the data is not as important as understanding the different types of data available to you and how you can use them.

Master Schedule Data

Class Size. You can use class size data to balance teachers' class loads, reduce or eliminate sections that are not at full capacity, or add a subject or course that will have more interest for more students. We have used these data to trim the "fluff," or underenrolled classes, in the master schedule and give teachers of common grade levels or subjects more time to collaborate on instructional practices, curriculum, and assessments. In some cases, we have combined several underenrolled courses (such as three levels of art) in the same period or moved the more advanced students in a general education class to an honors class.

Course Continuation. Course continuation data can help you determine the value of maintaining certain courses. For example, at one middle school we worked with, the staff debated whether or not to continue to offer Latin to students. Many staff members believed that the class was a waste of allocated staffing. The course continuation data, however, revealed a different story: approximately 90 percent of the students who took the course continued taking Latin when they went to high school. Each year, the staff revisited these data to determine whether or not to continue the Latin program at the middle school level. Course continuation data can be very useful, but we offer a caveat: if your staff members believe that these data are being used solely to justify the removal of classes, they will start to be apprehensive of data discussions.

Special Education. These data can help you not only determine the resources and accommodations that special education students will need throughout the year but also examine the number of students with special needs in each class and identify areas where teachers might need additional support or supplies. A longitudinal look at the number of students

Data abound in your school; the question is, Which data do you want, and how will you use them?

coming to your school or moving from one grade level to the next can help you identify any increase in the number of students with individualized education programs (IEPs) or 504 plans. You might establish a goal of reducing that number as much as possible and appropriate while still maintaining focus on these students' needs and success, regardless of accommodation documentation.

As Sharon Vaughn (2002) states, "Sadly, few children placed in special education close the achievement gap to a point where they can read and learn like their peers" (p. 7). She suggests that we "shift our focus on to making sure that individuals are getting the services that they need and away from the energy that's going into eligibility determination" (p. 26).

At one middle school we worked with, a central office staff member observed to the principal that there was a significant increase in students who had never had IEPs before suddenly beginning their middle school careers with IEPs. Data indicated a near–100 percent increase in IEPs from the feeder school to the next level. When the elementary school's special education staff members were asked about this astounding increase, they responded that they thought the students needed documented support to succeed in general education classes at the middle school level. Bringing these data to light sparked conversations based on objective information between the middle school and the elementary school general education and special education staff members. It turned out that the elementary teachers didn't believe the students could be successful without IEPs because middle school is just naturally more difficult than elementary school. This dialogue enabled middle school staff members to have a candid discussion with their elementary counterparts about readiness and universal skills as well as what kinds of resources and systematic supports were available at their school. The middle school staff members learned that they needed to find ways to better communicate to elementary school parents and staff that their students would not get lost in the shuffle without IEPs.

Gifted and Talented Education. Reviewing the demographics of gifted and talented, advanced placement, and honors classes can help you determine whether all students in your school are receiving equal access to enriched courses. You may discover that you have two different schools within one building: one with advanced courses taught predominantly to white students, and one with lower-level classes taught to a disproportionate number of minority students. In particular, we have seen this phenomenon in schools that were once predominantly white but shifted to reflect a more diverse population. Such schools, which often tout a diverse and integrated student body, are subject to "white flight" to advanced courses. If the data reveal such an imbalance in your school, you may want to encourage minority students to enroll in more advanced courses so that these classes' enrollments better reflect your school's overall student population and so that minority students have the same access to a rigorous curriculum.

You might also want to examine who teaches these courses. What do these data reveal? What message do students receive if only certain teachers teach advanced courses?

Administrative Data

Walk-Through. Walk-through data have several useful applications. For example, we have used them to ensure that we met our goals of conducting a certain number of walk-throughs each semester. Tracking these data on a weekly basis helped us maintain balance in our administrative schedules and avoid a backlog at the end of the semester. We have also used the data to identify which teachers, departments, and areas of the building we visited most, so that we could better spread out our efforts and visibility.

In some schools we worked in, we had teachers take attendance electronically, period by period, to provide ongoing attendance information throughout the day. We examined the data to determine where we might conduct walk-throughs to help teachers identify methods to reduce tardiness.

You can also share data from walk-throughs with teacher teams to provide tallies of certain observable behaviors and instructional practices (see Resource 11). Providing this information helps focus staff development efforts and identifies desirable norms to put in place in your school.

Peer Observation. If your school decides to implement peer observations, then you need to make sure the effort is executed as outlined for all staff. You can do this by keeping a weekly or biweekly tally of who has been observing and who has been observed (see Resource 8). We like to keep a simple spreadsheet like the one shown in Figure 7.1.

If you find that a certain teacher has not been participating, you can share these data when you bring up the issue to show that it is nothing personal. For example, you could note that according to the data, he or she is not among the 70 percent of staff members

Figure 7.1	Sample Peer Observation Spreadsheet			
Name	Date Observing	Observing Whom	Date Observed	Observed by Whom
Brown	9/10/07	O'Toole	10/17/07	Fields
Fields	10/17/07	Brown	9/27/07	Miller
Hernandez	10/10/07	Miller	11/9/07	O'Toole
Miller	9/27/07	Fields	10/10/07	Hernandez
O'Toole	11/9/07	Hernandez	9/10/07	Brown

who have completed their observation responsibilities and ask, "When can I add you to the completed list?" You can also use the peer observation data to identify best practices to share throughout the building.

Book Checkout. Librarians have all kinds of data, but they are not often asked to share them at the school level. You should determine how regularly books are being checked out and whether teachers are using the library resources with their students. If your analyses of circulation rates and library reservation time reveal that they are not, you should publicize these data and discuss them with staff to determine the reason for the lack of usage.

You should also review the degree to which teachers check out professional literature. One school we worked with that decided to assign a book to the entire faculty for professional development saved money by not purchasing a copy for every staff member but instead obtaining a class set to be housed in the library. The inventory data allowed the leadership to determine whether the purchase was a good investment that should be repeated for other schoolwide staff development efforts.

Equipment Checkout. Schools interested in infusing technology into their curricula might find these data beneficial. For example, one school we worked at purchased 70 personal response systems and kept them in the library. School leadership tracked their usage and created a bar graph showing how the usage increased throughout the year. At the end of the year, some teachers requested more personal response systems, but the data did not indicate that the school needed more units. We found that there was great demand for the units during the first two periods on Tuesday and Thursday but that the units were hardly ever used on Monday, Wednesday, or Friday. Instead of buying more, we evened out the schedule of usage. We also asked those who frequently checked out a set for their class activities to demonstrate examples of how they were incorporating the systems in their classes at faculty meetings. This resulted in increased usage the following year, which justified additional purchases at that time.

Teacher Data

Teacher Attendance. The media have recently heightened their focus on the issue of teacher absence, especially in the wake of recent studies by Harvard University and Duke University (Keller, 2008), and who can blame them? If teachers are not present to teach, students cannot learn, especially when substitutes are used to keep classes in a holding pattern until the teacher returns. You can pull attendance data to identify which teachers tend to take off on weekend bookends and determine which departments or teams have high rates of absenteeism. Once you have identified certain patterns, you can address the issue with other leaders who are in an evaluative capacity at the school and district levels.

Teacher Satisfaction. Opinion surveys are a good way to gather information about teacher satisfaction. Surveys offer much more structure and objectivity than workroom gossip or complaints. After the survey results are tallied, teachers can join in brainstorming ways to improve work satisfaction. More satisfied teachers often result in more satisfied students, parents, and administrators.

Teacher Turnover. The degree of teacher turnover can, naturally enough, correlate with the degree of teacher satisfaction. You might want to analyze the ratio of mentors to novice teachers and ask the novices to evaluate their mentors. Analyzing the results of such a survey can be especially helpful for you in strengthening this important role. Providing new teachers with a strong support structure is one of the keys to reducing teacher turnover.

Student Data

Extracurricular Involvement. Studies have shown that students who are involved in the life of the school are more likely to earn good grades and stay out of trouble (Broh, 2002; Smith, 1994). You should determine through student surveys and by talking with your sponsors, advisors, and coaches how many students participate in clubs and athletics and brainstorm ways to get more students involved (see Resource 19).

Student Satisfaction. You can determine the level of student satisfaction by surveying current students or a sample population of students who have left your school. We have used this information to guide our efforts around student services, student hospitality, course selection, rules, attendance of off-campus educational opportunities, and interventions. Leslye Abrutyn (2006) discusses ways to gather data from students and use them to set new goals. Examples of survey questions she provides include

- What are your class's goals?
- What are you learning?
- Why are you learning this particular lesson?
- Did last year's class prepare you to be successful this year?

Food Consumption. It might sound strange to analyze food consumption, but some staff members at a middle school we worked with noticed that students' academic performance and level of engagement declined between the morning and the afternoon. They attributed the decline to a combination of fatigue and poor eating habits during lunch and decided to gather data on food consumption to test their hypothesis.

Teachers and students analyzed cafeteria sales receipts of food purchased by a control group and also examined what brown-bagging students packed in their lunches. The staff used this information to develop an interdisciplinary lesson about the benefits of a healthy diet and identified ways to measure the students' performance in relation to their diet. Overall, the study and lesson were well received by students and parents, and the teachers saw some improvement in students' eating choices and class participation.

Discipline. Student discipline data can tell you what kinds of infractions are most prevalent and reveal any correlations between certain types of infractions and particular demographics or grade levels. In addition, this information can help you identify teachers who have a higher-than-average rate of referrals and discipline issues and to target problem periods and areas of the building. You can also use these data to develop training to help staff better manage disciplinary issues.

Absence. This is an obvious area to target: if students aren't in class, they aren't learning. Schools should use absence data to set goals to improve overall attendance rates as well as attendance for problem grade levels, courses, demographics, and times of year. You can address student absenteeism by sending letters home, making phone calls to family, holding conferences, making truancy referrals, removing privileges, and so on.

D–F **Grades.** Reducing the number of low and failing grades should be a priority for any school. You can pull grade distributions by teacher, class, subject, and department to open a discussion about assessments and grading practices and about why some students aren't achieving at a higher level.

Final Grades for Incoming Students. Reviewing the final grades of rising students can help you conduct a needs assessment for that class. If students have a lot of *A*s, you may need to consider an increase in advanced classes, whereas a high number of *F*s could indicate a need for additional remediation. As administrators, we used these data in discussions with teachers about grading policies and about how students fare when they reach the next grade level. In meetings with administrative teams from multiple schools, we have discussed strategies to ease students' transition from one school to the next. We have also used these data to provide guidance on staff development days for teachers who teach a common subject area at different grade levels. During these sessions, the data provided a foundation for discussing vertical curriculum alignment.

Establish the Value of Data

Educational leaders often tell us that they recognize the value of data but are unsure of how and when they can help staff see their value as well. We suggest first presenting data that show an area in which the school, department, or team seems to excel. This is an excellent entry point for establishing the value of data: even those who don't care for data will feel pride in seeing a statistic that indicates some level of success or growth. But simply showing staff these positive data are not enough; you need an example that you can turn on its ear.

For example, we once worked with a suburban middle school with a primarily white student population. No one had ever indicated to teachers that the generally successful school had had any problems. We were new to the school and needed to find a way to tell the staff that the school had areas in critical need of improvement—specifically, that subgroups were passing standardized assessments at a significantly lower rate than the general population. To begin the conversation, we focused on the passing rate for the Virginia Standards of Learning (SOL) writing test. The school was rightfully proud of its 91 percent passing rate on this high-stakes test. When teachers saw these data, many exclaimed, "Of course we're doing well! We know that!"

> When looking at data, one of the most important questions you can ask is, "Why?"

Our next step was to show how drilling deeper into the data can reveal more about a school than the staff generally knows. We shared a graph displaying the same SOL data disaggregated by demographic (see Figure 7.2), and the results suddenly looked very different. Starkly revealed was the fact that black students, who accounted for only 7 percent of the school population, had a passing rate of 56 percent and accounted for 37 percent of the failing SOL scores.

Clearly, breaking down the data revealed something that faculty members were previously unaware of: they were not as successful as they had thought. We did not present these data to attack them but to show them how data can bring hidden facts and trends to light.

One teacher, feeling defensive, questioned the value of highlighting such a small group of students: "I am not sure why we are

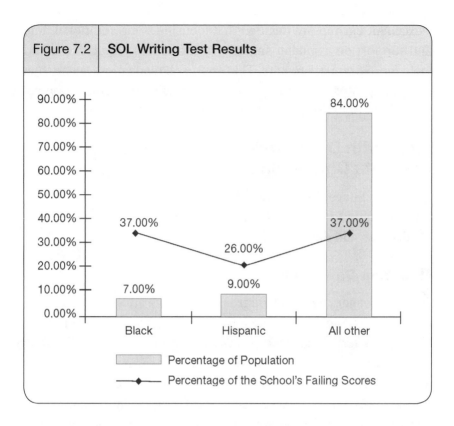

Figure 7.2 | SOL Writing Test Results

Percentage of Population
Percentage of the School's Failing Scores

so focused on so few students when we are doing so well!" Some staff members nodded in agreement. We responded, "If you were the parent of a black child and had this information, would you want to enroll her in our school knowing that she has only a 56 percent possibility of passing a required state assessment?"

This question was met with a long, awkward silence. We followed up by observing, "Of course your answer is no, but if we are wrong, please say so." We then addressed the entire group: "So now, what are we as a group of professionals going to do about the situation?" By following up in this way, we avoided the pitfall of presenting data for the sake of presenting data. Data are a tool that show us where and when to take action. In this case, data helped us illustrate that 16 percent of the student population (Hispanic as well as black students) owned 63 percent of the school's failing scores. As a group, we decided that focusing some additional time and support on a smaller segment of the school population could yield more dramatic results. This approach made more sense than scattering the school's limited resources over the entire population and hoping for the best outcome.

Work with Data Challengers and Data Champions

As you facilitate discussions about data with your staff, you will quickly come to see two broad categories of professionals: data challengers and data champions.

Meet Your Data Challengers

Data challengers generally distrust data. Some are simply unaccustomed to the idea of using data to analyze and improve their practice; others fear what the data might tell them. Still others believe that standardized testing is not the best measure of proficiency and as a result do not value the data they yield, despite the fact that schools are evaluated according to these data. Many think using data is yet another educational fad that will soon fade away. Here is how you can address your school's data challengers.

Disarm Data Concerns. Some data challengers have no experience reviewing and making use of data; others have had only bad experiences. Many fear the prospect of data being manipulated to show what someone wants them to show, of being evaluated according to the data, or of data being made available for public consumption. Some teachers may have fallen victim in the past to poor decisions made on the basis of good data, or to good decisions made on the basis of bad data. Perhaps they were shut out of the data analysis, or they received no support in interpreting and translating the data into meaningful action plans. Some data challengers haven't personally suffered from the misapplication of data but have heard about other people's bad experiences through the grapevine.

Whatever the source of challengers' distrust of data, confirmation rather than outright dismissal is the best strategy for allaying their concerns. Open a dialogue by acknowledging that data can be manipulated or misinterpreted; then openly vow that you will not base decisions on data without close, careful analysis of both the source of the data and the method of compiling the results.

Don't make judgments based on opinion; use data to avoid personal conflict of opinions.

As for teachers who are concerned that data will reflect poorly on their practice, offer the following scenario for them to ponder: when their own child is preparing to go back to school and they discover which teacher he or she will have, are they ever disappointed? Have they ever requested that their child be moved from one teacher's class to another's? Most would probably admit to knowing whom they did and didn't want their children to have as a teacher. Most of the time, their opinions have less to do with reviewing actual data on proficiency levels than with hearing other parents or neighborhood children recounting a negative experience with that teacher. The point you should drive home is that information about teachers' effectiveness is not confidential. In most cases, there are no surprises: the struggling teacher generally knows that he or she is struggling without ever having seen comparison data. And parents of children in that teacher's class may well know that the teacher is struggling without having seen official data to support their conjecture.

Once you have broached this subject, help your staff understand that the main purpose of data analysis is to identify ways to improve practice, not to punish or even to evaluate. Of course, if assessment results indicate that students are performing below expectations, teachers will want to see their students improve. When data shed light on a problem, you should have teachers submit a plan of action to improve their students' learning and, ultimately, their assessment data. We have yet to find struggling teachers who want to stay that way; however, educational leaders often tell underperforming teachers that they need to improve their teaching skills without providing specifics for them to focus on—a directive similar to your teachers telling their students, "You need to get better. I don't have any advice for you, but you can see that you need to improve right away, so be sure to fix it!" When you frame the discussion in terms of wanting to support teachers in specific, identified areas of need, you will be able to reassure them of the use of data.

Another way to help staff become more comfortable with the idea of data is to use them as a source for celebrations. Every time student performance improves or teachers meet a goal, share the data, then celebrate the achievement. In this way, data confirm to teachers that they are making a difference. Positive recognition makes the data something that teachers look forward to seeing rather than numbers that tell them they aren't doing what they should be doing.

Reassure Data Challengers. Here are some suggestions to reassure your data challengers:

- Recognize and make use of challengers' strengths.
- Encourage challengers to engage in discussions around data and to share possible solutions to problems that data reveal.
- Take advantage of challengers' tendency to be critical; let them know you look forward to their critiques and their creativity in problem solving.
- Encourage challengers to open up about their distrust of data without the fear of retaliation. Be sure to provide structure to these conversations to avoid gripe sessions; the objective is to gain buy-in from the challengers and identify solutions.
- Include the challengers in staff development discussions.
- Help allay fears by starting with light data, such as attendance, graduation rates, and incoming students' grades. In

time, deepen the conversations with more pointed, personal data on such issues as the rate of *D*s and *F*s, common assessments, and discipline.

• Pair your data challengers with your data champions during data team meetings and other data discussions and reviews; use newly converted data champions to help challengers see the light of data.

If these approaches don't work with your data challengers, then you'll need to play the authority card. You can't sit on the sidelines watching one challenger derail the team. For example, we were once helping a team of high school teachers identify data they could use to guide them in developing goals for their curriculum teams. During this workshop, we referred to research and best practices identified by Robert Marzano, Douglas Reeves, Rick Stiggins, and a few others. During one of the breaks, an advanced placement teacher asked for a moment off the record and stated that she had never seen the value of data. She explained, "We come to work and we do what we are good at; the rest is up to the student." She closed her position by saying that she didn't believe in wasting time collaborating with other teachers or reviewing data.

This was not the first time we had encountered this type of resistance. We responded by asking her to imagine that she needed a medical procedure on her brain. Would she choose the doctor who worked in isolation, refusing to collaborate with other doctors or keep up with current research and data? Or would she prefer the doctor who used all the resources available to stay up-to-date with the latest medical advances? She said that we had twisted the issue because if it were brain surgery, of course she would want the most current approaches. Our response to her and to all data challengers: if you would expect the best and most current practices when someone is working on your brain, why would you hold yourself to a lower standard when working with children's brains?

Meet Your Data Champions

Data champions promote the use of data to inform decision making and evaluation. They embrace data because they are objective and enable them to operate more scientifically, without letting emotions or personal preferences cloud their judgment. These teachers use data both to promote improvement efforts and to deflect others' challenges to those efforts.

Empower Your Data Champions. As a school leader, you should identify the data champions in your building and encourage them to serve on the team that develops the school improvement plan. Court their involvement by explaining how advantageous it would be to have them on the team to help others fully understand the power and usefulness of data. A little sincere flattery can go a long way to secure their involvement! Here are some other ways for you to get the most out of your data champions:

- Ask them for guidance on data-related issues whenever possible.
- Encourage them to teach colleagues how to review, analyze, and make decisions based on data, citing real-life examples of how they use data.
- Give them an opportunity to share concerns about data that they hear from other staff.
- Recruit them to help address and allay staff members' data-related concerns.
- Draw on their strengths to lead and enrich discussions on data.
- Brainstorm with them to identify other sources of data in the building and how to use them.
- Results are the breakfast of data champions, so make sure to keep your champions happy by "feeding" them data and data-related projects.

Track and Share Data

When working with data—specifically standardized test results—
too many schools and educators are satisfied with asking a single
question: "How did we do?" It's natural for teachers to want to
know how their students performed on the latest battery of standardized tests. But it's time to replace "How did we do?" with "How
are we doing?" We need to continually track and analyze data and
examine the trends that they reveal, not just wait for a final snap-
shot at the end of a course. When examining data, you should ask
(and encourage your teachers to ask) the following questions:

- Is there an upward trend?
- Is there a downward trend?
- Is the trend flat?
- Is there a curve?
- Is there a reverse curve?
- Is the trend erratic?

These questions are important ones. You might introduce them
to staff by saying, "You can't know where you are unless you know
where you've been." If you look at data only once or in isolation at
the end of a course or school year, you might learn where you are
that day, but you really have no way of knowing whether you are
gaining or losing ground.

An upward trend (see Figure 7.3) can indicate a steady rate of
improvement. It's possible that you don't need to make significant
modifications. However, just because the line is headed in the right
direction does not mean improvement is not necessary. The trend
may reveal that progress is not occurring according to the desired
timeline, for example.

A downward trend (see Figure 7.4) obviously indicates a need
for improvement. You and your staff should pay particular attention to how large and how rapid the drop is. These details indicate

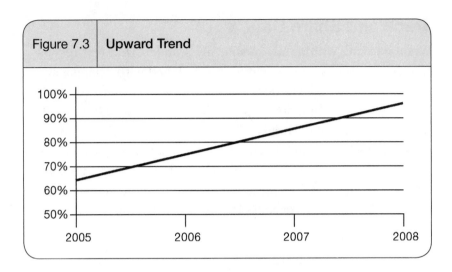

Figure 7.3 | Upward Trend

the degree of importance of the change, which can help you priori-tize areas of focus.

A flat trend (see Figure 7.5), for better or for worse, indicates consistent performance. You should engage teachers in a dialogue about whether or not this flat performance is acceptable and iden-tify whether they can improve (and if so, how), or whether they have reached saturation and have achieved as much as they can.

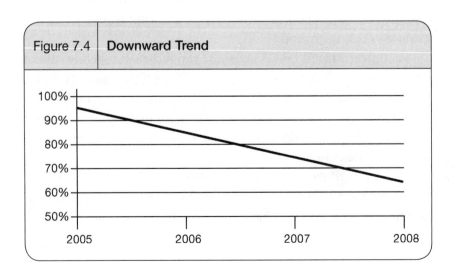

Figure 7.4 | Downward Trend

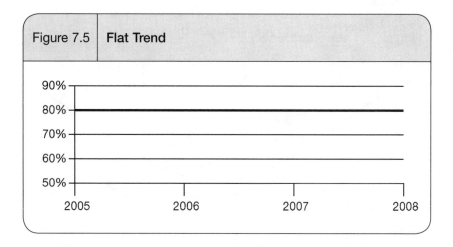

Figure 7.5 | Flat Trend

A curve (see Figure 7.6) indicates that something has changed significantly enough to change an upward trend into a sudden downward trend. You might look at whether there have been changes in personnel, student demographics, methods of curriculum delivery, or assessment instruments to help you develop a hypothesis about the reason for the decline.

A reverse curve (see Figure 7.7) indicates that you have been down but are now on your way up. You may want to discuss what has changed or what is currently being done differently to maintain this upward trend.

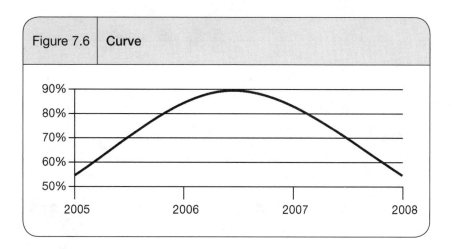

Figure 7.6 | Curve

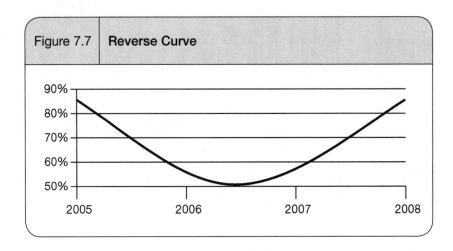

Figure 7.7 | Reverse Curve

When you see an erratic trend (see Figure 7.8), you and your staff should work to figure out what caused both the upward and the downward trend and identify how to avoid future declines while maintaining the growth.

You want your teachers to see these data as their collective data, coming from their school, themselves and their colleagues, their students, and their community. Make sure to continually share data with staff members so that they become accustomed to the idea that everyone owns the data. We recommend starting the

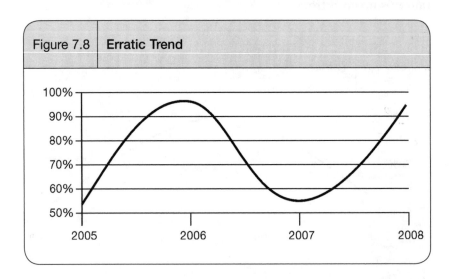

Figure 7.8 | Erratic Trend

year by distributing data packets to the entire faculty and using the first meeting to discuss and analyze the data. You should also provide data updates throughout the year at faculty meetings.

Standardized achievement tests yield a considerable amount of data, so you might want to distribute responsibility for tracking the data. For example, after test results arrive in the building, assistant principals could pull the data for the departments or grade levels they supervise and provide unfiltered data to their teacher leaders. The teacher leaders could then disseminate the data to their respective teams or departments, making sure to protect the privacy of individual teachers as much as possible. Ms. Jones does not need to know how Mr. Smith's class has done on an assessment. Instead, teacher leaders should provide their departments with overall passing rates on subjects and content strands disaggregated by demographics.

Teacher leaders could create data walls in their workrooms by posting pertinent data for the entire department to see. Another way to share data is through data rooms (Waiksnis, 2008). Data rooms are central locations like the mail room or the copy room where you can post data—again, as long as they are not confidential and do not identify students and teachers by name. As Waiksnis notes, "It takes time to do this, but I want my teachers implementing data-driven instruction, not trying to pull and compile information. I can do that part for them!" You don't have to limit the data you post to standardized test results. Waiksnis explains that "we track discipline referrals, attendance, tardies, and anything else we can quantify. All in all, the numbers are posted for them to see on a daily basis. My goal is to keep the numbers out there, not tucked away in a binder on a bookshelf." Sharing is free, and the more you share, the more likely it is that teachers will use the data.

Use Data to Make Decisions

After tracking, sharing, and analyzing data, you need to determine whether staff can use them to make improvements. Data are only helpful when they are specific and relevant and reveal issues that staff can actually address. It is also essential to identify a baseline of the data and a goal for the desired change. Without these criteria, the discussions around data could lead to minimal outcomes (see Resource 20).

Data also need to be timely to be useful. Standardized test results from the spring being returned to teachers the following fall are not timely, for example. Although these data are important and provide feedback that teachers can use to identify trends and patterns from one year or group of students to the next, their late delivery prevents teachers from using them in the most direct way: with the actual cohort of students tested. An example of timely data would be interim grades. A teacher who has a high number of failing students in her class during that reporting period can develop a plan of action to change the results for that group of students.

We once worked with an English department in a suburban high school that was attempting to improve its state standardized test scores. The department chair first presented the state's testing data and led a discussion in which teachers identified the specific state learning standards and the essential skills that all students needed to learn. The teachers then pinpointed areas of weakness in student results on content-area strands, not only examining overall passing rates but also looking at how students performed on specific groups of skill and content questions. The data enabled them to develop strategies to ensure that students would obtain and retain the needed skills. When the department chair presented several years of data on specific strands, the teachers decided to revise their method of delivering content—specifically, to increase their emphasis on areas showing downward and flat trends. They built in extra time for this by reducing their focus on content strands that showed upward trends.

If dialogues around data are new for your school, it may be easier to start discussing data with more receptive teams or departments.

After experiencing an improvement in standardized test scores, the department decided to review its grading scales and practices to ensure rigor and consistency. Some teachers believed there might be some discrepancies between students' assigned grades and their performance on the standardized tests. They decided to first compare and analyze the students' grade averages without relation to the standardized test scores, compiling three separate sets of data as shown in Figure 7.9: T GPA, MP2 GPA, and Cum GPA. T GPA refers to the grade point average of all of each teacher's students for the second marking period; MP2 GPA refers to *all* of each student's grades from the second marking period; and Cum GPA refers to each student's cumulative grade point average of record.

Each teacher received a copy of this graph with his or her own name marked below the appropriate bars. This allowed the teachers to see how they stood in comparison with other teachers and with the department average. Only the administration and the department chair had a graph with all the teacher names listed. Before distributing the chart, the department chair and the administrator emphasized that the data were not a tool to use to judge others, especially because many of the teachers had never received this type of data before. Once the chart was distributed and explained, staff members asked questions about how the data were compiled.

Most of the department members agreed that ideally, the three data points shown in Figure 7.9 should be relatively closely aligned. The teachers also discussed the fact that their department, being a core academic area, taught all the students in the school and therefore was able to get the most accurate averages. This kind of discussion is helpful because some teachers are less well versed than others in reviewing data.

We also discussed how we could use discrepancies between data points to examine and improve measurements of student learning and grading practices. Some teachers worried that if everyone knew the target average score, teachers could just pad their grades or adjust their grading policies to achieve the desired balance. Through discussion, they realized that predicting the

Figure 7.9 | Department Data with Three Data Points

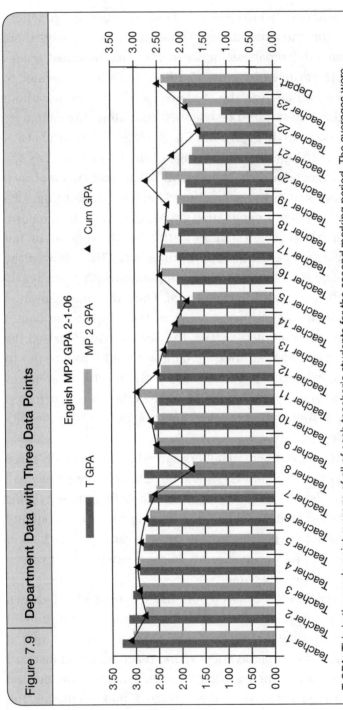

T GPA: This is the grade point average of all of each teacher's students for the second marking period. The averages were computed by converting each student's letter grade for that period to a numerical value and averaging the numerical values. $A = 4, B = 3, C = 2, D = 1, F = 0$.

MP 2 GPA: This figure was derived using the same formula used to calculate the T GPA, but based on *all* of each student's grades from the second marking period.

Cum GPA: This is each student's cumulative grade point average of record. This figure was calculated starting with each student's first high school credit class (most often 9th grade, but some from earlier grade levels).

average would be impossible, since that figure would be reached by averaging together all students' grades, which would be impossible for an individual teacher to predict or control. Therefore, it would be impossible for teachers to scale their grades to match the undetermined department average. The discussion was encouraging: everyone recognized that there was no way for anyone to be set up to look good or bad.

As teachers' comfort level increased, some of them started sharing which bars they represented on the chart. This trust and openness marked the beginning of a powerful discussion about grading practices. Teacher 8 mentioned to the group that he had graded a little more leniently than some of his colleagues had because many of his students were classified as special education. His grading and assessment practices sparked a discussion about special education students in a regular education classroom receiving accommodations but having to pass the same state assessment. Many of this teacher's special education students were receiving Bs but weren't demonstrating anything close to the same level of proficiency on the state assessment. The disconnect between their course grades and their standardized assessment scores brought to light the difficulty of improvement: how could students know which skills they needed to improve on?

On the flipside, teacher 11 observed that her students' cumulative GPAs and marking period GPAs were fairly good and was concerned that she was grading too hard. Throughout these discussions, department members agreed that they should have a common baseline method of determining student grades. They agreed that both students and teachers would benefit from more consistent assessment and grading practices across classes, especially for common courses taught by different teachers.

The clear, objective data provided by this graph enabled the department to engage in a highly productive, meaningful meeting. Although administrators compiled the data and created the graph, they did not dominate the meeting. Instead, the department chair

If you give teachers good data and time to digest their meaning, most of the time they will make good use of the data.

. . . .

brought the department to consensus, developed action plans with the department, and created follow-up staff development based on the data.

Another important data set to consider is how students fared on high-stakes assessments (in Virginia, the SOL, where 400 is a passing score) in comparison with their final grades in the corresponding class (see Figure 7.10, pp. 190–191). For example, using a process similar to the one we previously discussed, you could supply teachers with an Excel spreadsheet that includes their students' high-stakes scores coupled with their final course grades. You could also supply a department with data that reflect high-stakes test scores in comparison with a teacher's classes' average (see Figure 7.11, p. 192).

Examining standardized assessment and course data can generate discussions about possible disconnects among curriculum, instruction, and assessment and how a department might adapt them for the future. We have worked with teachers who for the first time began analyzing student performance on various measures, asking the simple question "Why?" when presented with data that were not parallel, and developing hypotheses to explain what the data seemed to indicate.

These deep data analyses enable teachers to reflect year after year on how they assess students. For example, several teachers we worked with realized that they based their grades more on major projects, such as presentations and group work, than on test performance. They realized that they had to achieve a better balance between alternative assessments and more traditional ones. They started developing common formative assessments that adhered to the state tests' format both to expose students to the kinds of assessments they would need to pass for promotion and to receive better feedback on their students' needs.

Develop Formative Assessments

Formative assessments yield powerful data that teachers can use to guide their instructional practices. These data need to be precise and meaningful enough to help educators identify specific areas of need, so you and your staff must disaggregate the data and drill down to specific skill areas. Your responsibility as a leader is to help teachers develop assessments that will deliver the data they need to assess and improve their practice and their students' performance.

Many schools decide to purchase premade and preloaded (i.e., content-included) assessment software packages. Although these packages have their benefits, doing it yourself saves money and helps teachers gain a better understanding of their state's objectives, standards, testing format, and proficiency requirements. A reliance on outside prepackaged assessments often precludes full teacher buy-in: if teachers use a product that they did not help create and do not get the results they had anticipated, they may believe that there is not much they can do about it except wait for the next product to come out.

Assessment packages do have some advantages, and they don't have to have a financial impact on your school if you are willing to think outside the box. At Thoreau Middle School in Fairfax County, Virginia, principal Mark Greenfelder wanted to develop formative assessments with his teachers that would deliver meaningful data about their students. He established a relationship with an executive at Northrop Grumman and discussed the possibility of collaborating to develop an assessment program for his teachers to use. After several meetings, they reached an agreement: Northrop Grumman would develop a software program with the input of the teachers at Thoreau, who would describe to the programmers exactly what they needed in terms of a formative assessment. The initial partnership was formed with Thoreau at no cost, and it later evolved into an agreement that included much of the school system. Such a strong and valuable partnership could not have been realized

Figure 7.10		SOL Scores Compared with Course Grades									
LN	FN	SOL Test	Grd	Teacher	Course	Student ID	Mark	SOL Score	Pts	Eth	Sex
Smith	Robert	History	8	Lynn	Civics	756713	A	489	4	1	M
Garcia	Jose	History	8	Lynn	Civics	808625	B+	489	3.5	3	M
Nguyen	Brian	History	8	Lynn	Civics	826444	B	473	3	5	M
Daniels	Thomas	History	8	Lynn	Civics	832685	C	465	2	1	M
Kennedy	William	History	8	Lynn	Civics	765128	B	453	3	1	M
Alexander	Laytoya	History	8	Lynn	Civics	738962	B	453	3	2	F
Dade	Mary	History	8	Lynn	Civics	765755	B+	448	3.5	1	F
Moore	John	History	8	Lynn	Civics	774163	C+	433	2.5	1	M
Davis	Shareeka	History	8	Lynn	Civics	738310	C	414	2	2	F
McCarter	Paul	History	8	Lynn	Civics	807646	C+	406	2.5	1	M
Sylvester	Mariam	History	8	Lynn	Civics	804071	C+	402	2.5	1	F
France	Cassie	History	8	Lynn	Civics	749086	B+	394	3.5	1	F
McDaniel	Pete	History	8	Lynn	Civics	765798	C	394	2	2	M
Romero	Sylvia	History	8	Lynn	Civics	774722	B	382	3	3	F
Johnson	Missy	History	8	Lynn	Civics	765514	B	382	3	1	F

Figure 7.10	SOL Scores Compared with Course Grades (continued)

LN	FN	SOL Test	Grd	Teacher	Course	Student ID	Mark	SOL Score	Pts	Eth	Sex
Taylor	Jaunita	History	8	Lynn	Civics	738962	B	378	3	2	F
Stein	Gregory	History	8	Lynn	Civics	857783	C+	378	2.5	1	M
Gibbons	Albert	History	8	Lynn	Civics	779159	C+	370	2.5	1	M
Barahona	Maria	History	8	Lynn	Civics	713110	B	365	3	3	F
Wynn	Dwayne	History	8	Lynn	Civics	807056	C	361	2	3	M
Bates	Kevin	History	8	Lynn	Civics	773774	B	343	3	2	M
Contreras	Cynthia	History	8	Lynn	Civics	806917	B	338	3	3	F
Rodriguez	Julio	History	8	Lynn	Civics	818298	C	338	2	3	M
						Average		406.43	2.78		

Legend:
LN = Student's last name
FN = Student's first name
SOL Test = Content of assessment
Grd = Grade level of student
Teacher = Teacher name
Course = Name of course of study

Student ID = Student identification
  number
Mark = Grade assigned to student that
  marking period
SOL Score = Student score on the
  assessment

Pts = Mark converted to a numeric
  value (A = 4, B+ = 3.5, B = 3, etc.)
Eth = Ethnic coding to indicate the
  student's registered ethnicity
Sex = Sex of student

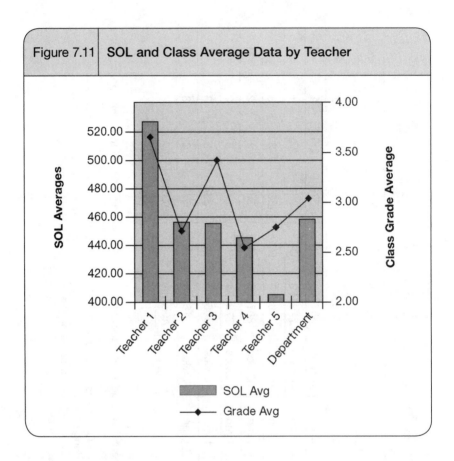

Figure 7.11 | SOL and Class Average Data by Teacher

without Greenfelder's creative leadership and the school's willingness to challenge the norm of spending to solve problems and instead seeking support and opportunities within the community.

Obtain Content and Format Information

If the goal of your school's formative assessments is to improve results on high-stakes assessments, then you need to obtain the information necessary to create formative assessments whose data work for you. Some states make this task a little easier than others; for example, Virginia, Ohio, Texas, Massachusetts, North Carolina, and several other states provide extensive, specific information on their standards or objectives and skills—sometimes called *essential skills* or *essential knowledge*.

If your state does not publicly post this type of information, you or an appointed staff member can perform some basic research. The first step is to call the state department of education for the information. Consider asking the following questions:

Make use of the "researchers" on your staff: they like investigating and probing for information, and they are usually good at it.

....

- Can you tell me where I can find the blueprint for the state assessment in [grade level and subject]?

- Will the blueprint provide me with the number of questions or weight of each standard, or at least the reporting area that will be assessed on the state assessment?

- Where can I find the essential skills that a student needs to possess to demonstrate proficiency on all of the questions that will be on the state assessment?

If they don't have these answers, you need to be persistent and ask who could provide them. All the while, you should emphasize how important it is to you that your students are successful on this year's battery of assessments. If your conversation still does not produce results, then ask which vendor develops the assessments. This is free public information because taxpayer money was involved. The next step is to find out which other states have employed this vendor and check whether those states post the information you are seeking. The information might not be identical to your state's, but it would at least be more information than you have already.

Help Teachers Use Results to Inform Their Practice

Once your teachers have identified the framework they want their formative assessments to follow, they are ready to begin constructing assessments that will provide meaningful data. When creating formative assessments, it is important for you as a leader to help them understand why they need to keep them to a manageable yet powerful size.

For example, a traditional assessment in a 10th grade biology class is typically a test consisting of 50 or 60 questions at the completion of each unit. When the teacher returns the test to his or her students, they know their scores and maybe the class average. The teacher knows the same—no more, no less. Short, regular, formative assessments throughout the unit, on the other hand, provide more information and do a better job of guiding instruction. For example, one department we worked with developed an assessment consisting of 12 questions covering three concepts from the last three class sessions: cell structures and functions, plant and animal cellular differences, and diffusion and osmosis. Each topic was allotted four questions.

After the assessment, each student received his or her results, which provided specific information on each one of the areas tested. The student knew where he or she stood in each area, and the teachers were able to use the data to develop support action plans and to guide their ensuing instruction. If there is a high degree of trust and comfort on a team, teachers identify their own areas of strength and need and can talk with their colleagues about how they delivered the curriculum in classes that demonstrated higher proficiency.

Compiling assessment results is helpful in identifying any pockets of missing comprehension. Figure 7.12 (pp. 196–197) shows a chart created by a teacher in this department who taught three sections of biology. Each student received a number that corresponded alphabetically to his or her last name; most grade books, electronic or otherwise, have numbered lines, which makes this easy. The teacher organized the table by concept; the highest score any student could achieve for each concept in that section was a 4, indicating that the student correctly answered all four questions for that topic.

The teacher generated the table using simple spreadsheet software—in this case, Microsoft Excel. At this school, we were able to export class lists from our student information system, and then all the teachers had to do was import data from a bubble-sheet scanner. If your school doesn't use such a scanner, teachers can simply add the information by hand. This method takes a little extra time, but if the assessments are short and frequent—which we strongly recommend—then these tables will be short and easy to create and discuss.

Some teachers may protest that they don't have time to learn how to use spreadsheets; we argue that teachers don't have time *not* to learn how to use technology effectively. Once the teachers we worked with started using this format, it became more of a habit than a chore. Many school systems now use assessment engines that generate easy-to-read reports. For our purposes, these products are fine as long as the teachers are the ones developing the assessments. Taking ownership assures teachers that the learning being measured is something they had an opportunity to discuss and agree on before the assessment was administered.

Note the instances in Figure 7.12 where students did well with some skills but not with others, and consider the fact that the class averages were pretty good but that some individual students were clearly struggling. For example, student 7 in period 5 obviously needed some assistance in the area of "plant and animal cellular differences," having answered only one question correctly. But if we were concerned only with class averages, then this student might not receive any additional support because his number would get lost in the fairly high average score of 3.40.

Teachers should provide students with their scores on each area of the assessment and on individual questions. Some of the teachers we worked with liked to give their students the class average so that students had comparison data just as the teachers had; however, we don't recommend showing students data that reveal how classes compare to one another.

Students can review their results to develop study goals and plans with their teacher, another student, or their parents, and teachers can use the results as a resource for remediation efforts.

Figure 7.12 Teacher-Made Formative Common Assessment Results

Student	Cell Structures and Functions			Plant and Animal Cellular Differences			Diffusion and Osmosis		
	Period 1	Period 3	Period 5	Period 1	Period 3	Period 5	Period 1	Period 3	Period 5
1	3	3	3	4	3	3	3	4	3
2	3	3	3	3	2	4	2	3	3
3	3	3	3	3	4	4	3	3	3
4	3	3	3	4	4	4	2	3	3
5	3	3	4	4	3	4	3	3	3
6	3	3	3	3	4	3	4	3	3
7	1	3	3	4	3	1	1	3	2
8	3	4	3	3	3	4	3	3	3
9	3	3	4	3	4	4	2	3	3
10	3	3	3	1	4	2	3	3	3

| Figure 7.12 | Teacher-Made Formative Common Assessment Results (continued) |

	Cell Structures and Functions			Plant and Animal Cellular Differences			Diffusion and Osmosis		
Student	Period 1	Period 3	Period 5	Period 1	Period 3	Period 5	Period 1	Period 3	Period 5
11	3	3	3	4	3	3	3	3	1
12	3	3	4	4	3	3	1	3	3
13	3	3	3	2	4	4	1	3	3
14	3	4	3	3	3	4	3	3	3
15	3	3	3	4	4	3	2	3	3
16	3	3	3	4	3	3	2	3	3
17	4	3	3	3	3	3	3	3	3
18	3	3	4	4	3	4	1	2	3
19	3	-	3	3	-	4	1	-	3
20	-	-	3	-	-	4	-	-	3
Average	2.95	3.11	3.20	3.32	3.33	3.40	2.26	3.00	2.85

Many schools ensure that they have all the appropriate resources and personnel in place, but they don't put the most critical step in place: making sure that there is accurate information to guide these services. Those who provide remediation to students cannot be faulted for not achieving a high enough level of success if they aren't receiving specific information that tells them what to focus on with each student. For example, the results for student 7 in period 1 (see Figure 7.12) indicate that the student needs support only in the areas of cell structures and functions and diffusion and osmosis; this information would be very helpful to the person providing remediation. If teachers used only traditional, lengthy summative assessments, however, this important information would most likely get overlooked or not be provided in a timely manner.

Formative assessment results can also help teachers better differentiate their instruction. In heterogeneous classes, these data can help teachers with flexible ability groups. For example, for each of the three skill areas tested, teachers could group students with scores of 2 or below to better provide the support they need. They might also consider pairing students who did not excel in a given area with students who did excel in that area.

Use Assessment Results for Staff Development

Here comes the trickiest but most potentially rewarding part of reviewing both formative and standardized assessment results. If the team or department has developed a healthy, trusting culture, the potential for teachers' professional growth when they share and collaborate around data is almost limitless. Such educators will ask for their colleagues' feedback on their delivery of content and share specific strategies, activities, and ideas that will have a positive effect on students. For example, data revealing that one teacher's students have fared better with a particular skill or concept than other teachers' students would be an entry point for the teacher leader to facilitate some powerful professional conversations. This is not an opportunity for successful teachers to boast or belittle others, but rather a chance for everyone to learn something from one another. If your school has a healthy culture, teachers will express interest in how their colleagues get positive results and be anxious to see their students perform equally well. In one school we know, the teachers decided to laterally move struggling students to another class with better results as an immediate fix while the teachers figured out how to improve their professional practice as a team. We should point out that this solution was a temporary and unorthodox one that had the support of the principal and the parents.

Stretch Assessments

In one middle school we worked with, teachers developed pre-assessments containing questions on content that they planned to cover in the upcoming weeks. They explained to the students that the assessment results would help determine the amount of time they would spend on the different skills and objectives. This process saved teachers time because they found that they could trim time from certain areas in which the students already demonstrated proficiency. In this particular community, we identified a need for upfront communication with the parents, who were accustomed to their children bringing home assessment results of 90 percent or higher. Once we started including items covering not-yet-taught content, we adjusted our expectations to 70 percent for an overall assessment result with the least amount of demonstrated proficiency on the new skills. This initiative could have been a recipe for disaster if we had waited for students to take home results without communicating about the change in advance. Not all schools receive that level of parent involvement, but it's important to keep the lines of communication open as much as possible and offer families as much involvement as they'll accept.

> *Educators tend to want assessments to assess what was taught. To improve instructional efficiency, help them instead focus assessments on what was learned.*

The Cornerstone of Improvement

In schools that regularly use data to inform professional growth and goal setting, teachers' initial fear of data almost always subsides. In fact, after sharing and discussing data becomes an accepted practice, you will find staff hungry for more data. You and your teachers can use data to set goals on improving instruction, assessments, student learning, and staff development. As you start off on your data journey, keep the following points in mind:

- Data are objective: not good, not bad, just facts.
- Data remove opinions (and, as a result, personal feelings) from the decision-making process.
- Data do not criticize but illuminate.
- Data are a means toward continuous improvement.
- Data must be provided in an understandable, accessible format.
- Data should be analyzed to identify trends and patterns and strengths and weaknesses.
- Data should be cross-validated to ensure their accuracy.
- Data should be the foundation of decision making.
- Data are feedback, and feedback is our friend.
- Data must mean more than just averages.
- Data guide a staff's professional development.
- Data make the invisible visible.

Most important, data should be the cornerstone of all your improvement efforts. They are a key component to helping your school thrive.

Getting Started

- Not everyone will embrace data, so determine who your data champions are and recruit them to help convert your data challengers.
- There are different kinds of data available to you, so determine your priorities and what you hope to improve.
- Coach other leaders and teachers on how to analyze data.

Afterword

Helping a school thrive—especially without straining its budget—is a challenging task for even the most talented administrators and teacher leaders. As we have indicated throughout the book, leading change and transforming a school's culture must be a collective effort, just as teaching itself involves "moving from an individual to a collective activity" (Elmore & City, 2007, p. 3). And with so much at stake in these times of accountability, it makes sense to enlist the power and capacity of many to accomplish extraordinary tasks. School culture goes hand in hand with student achievement: rarely do schools with ill cultures produce positive results, and rarely do schools with healthy cultures produce poor results. The better you understand your school's culture, the better equipped you will be to transform it.

We believe that the norms and strategies we present in this book will help you get the most out of your school; they are purposeful and practical behaviors that will bring about increased achievement and efficacy for all stakeholders in the learning community. Once people start seeing improvement, they will be all the more likely to embrace such changes. But before your school reaches this point, there will be difficult times when progress is barely visible and stakeholders question the value of these changes. As Elmore and City (2007) note, "It feels horrible when you and your colleagues are working harder than you have ever worked, when you have accepted the challenge of incorporating new practices into your work with students, when you are participating in planning and collegial activities that force you to move outside your comfort zone—and you see no visible payoff for these huge investments." We mention this to reassure you when you face the inevitable "period(s) of flattened performance" (p. 1). It is a normal part of the improvement process. As we mentioned before, although the strategies we suggest cost little or no money, they do require an investment of time.

All change takes time, yet educators and administrators often expect instant results. When they do not see them, they often abandon whatever initiative or program they worked so hard to implement and quickly adopt a new one with similar promises of results. This creates a revolving door of initiatives that leads to unfocused, random, and eventually halfhearted and unsupported attempts at improvement. Do not embrace this all-too-common practice; instead, be mindful of the enduring "3 *P*s": Plan, Persistence, and Patience. You need a plan to move forward and accomplish any kind of change; improvement will not happen by accident. Persistence is important because you must be dedicated and committed to actualize your plan. Finally, patience is crucial: results take time. An important aspect of patience is understanding that there may be staff turnover during this process and that you should not be panicked by it; in many instances, turnover might actually be essential to the improvement process.

The strategies we provide in this book all lend themselves to "robust dialogue," which "brings reality to the surface through openness, candor, and informality" (Bossidy & Charan, 2002, p. 102). The key word here is *reality*. Many schools are unable to accept their current or future reality. Our recommendations are meant to assist you in dealing with this obstacle and in creating a culture where robust dialogue is the norm and a means toward improvement. As Bossidy and Charan (2002) note, "[R]obust dialogue makes an organization effective in gathering information, understanding the information, and reshaping it to produce decisions. It fosters creativity—most innovations and inventions are incubated through robust dialogue." They also observe that "robust dialogue brings out reality, even when that reality makes people uncomfortable. . . . It is open, tough, focused, and informal. The aim is to invite multiple viewpoints, see the pros and cons of each one, and try honestly and candidly to construct new viewpoints" (p. 102).

By establishing your school's vision, distributing leadership, and inviting others to participate in change, you are well on your way toward establishing a "dynamic that stimulates new questions, new ideas, and new insights rather than wasting energy on defending the old order" (Bossidy & Charan, 2002, p. 102). Because ultimately, it is not about what you have always done, but what you have yet to do.

Resource 1

A Framework for Discussing Culture

You and your staff can use this reference tool to help you assess your culture and open up a dialogue around acceptable and unacceptable practices and behaviors. Keep in mind that not all schools fall squarely in one category. Nevertheless, you should be able to get a feel for where your school falls on the spectrum.

	Indicators of a Healthy Culture	Indicators of a Benign Culture	Indicators of an Ill Culture
Leadership	The leadership framework functions both vertically and horizontally.	Leadership is visible and respected, but the school is not building leadership capacity.	Leadership is not respected and often appears dysfunctional, lacking follow-through and support from staff.
	Leadership is shared and distributed among key teachers. The staff is invited to participate in decision making when appropriate.	Leadership responsibilities are covered but at times appear to be coveted by administrators. Most decisions are accepted but are top-down.	Leadership is often perceived as working in isolation without seeking input from lead teachers or other professionals in the building, and the decisions are not supported by staff. Leadership is autocratic and top-down.
	There is a direct connection between espoused beliefs and administrative practices.	Administration follows shared beliefs and practices, but there is little to no input from the staff to identify and develop the beliefs and practices.	Administration appears not to have any consistent standards or values. The practices put in place are often not understood, supported, or followed by staff.
Meetings	Teams work in a collegial and collaborative fashion toward a shared, agreed-upon purpose.	Teams work respectfully and with purpose, but their meetings' main focus is to respond to directives.	Teams are identified by name, but there is little to no collaboration among members and no common understanding of the teams' purpose.

Meetings *(continued)*	Staff development is an integral part of team, department, and faculty meetings. Staff members identify needed staff development activities and administration provides the needed resources.	Staff development activities are chosen and provided to staff by administration.	Administration provides staff development when directed by central administration or a supervisor. Staff demonstrate considerable resistance in response to staff development activities.
	Meetings have clear protocols and practices that are developed collaboratively by all stakeholders and respected and maintained by all meeting participants.	Meetings are conducted in an orderly and routine fashion. Because participants did not agree on the protocols, the protocols will be tested at times and may go unaddressed, or staff will wait for the administration to address the issues.	Meetings lack structure. They are often held without defined outcomes and lack follow-up. Attendance is sporadic, side-bar conversations are frequent, and staff members resent mandated meetings.
	Meetings include cross-curricular team and department dialogues.	Team and department meetings are productive but work in isolation of one another.	Teams and departments meet because they are required to. Outcomes are random, and there is no cross-curricular dialogue.
Instruction	Instruction is articulated vertically and horizontally within subject areas.	Teachers follow a prescribed curriculum and keep focused on their subject and/or grade level alone.	Once the classroom door shuts, teachers are on their own. Isolation is acceptable and even desirable for some.

	Indicators of a Healthy Culture	Indicators of a Benign Culture	Indicators of an Ill Culture
Instruction *(continued)*	Teacher teams discuss and share varied activities and strategies, and the strategies are responsive to student needs.	Teachers use effective strategies, but professional sharing is limited and unstructured.	Teachers teach in their preferred styles. There is little instructional variety, and for many, the way they learned is the way they teach.
	Teachers develop and administer regular, thoughtful, common formative assessments on what students know and are able to do.	Quizzes and tests are administered on a regular basis but differ from one teacher to another.	Teachers individually develop summative assessments; formative assessments are almost unheard of in this culture.
	Reteaching and remediation are an important part of instruction and are based on the results of common formative assessments. Support for students is centralized and individualized.	Students receive reteaching and remediation on the basis of individual teacher assessments and requests.	It is the responsibility of the students to learn and meet expectations by paying attention. There are few, if any, remediation or reteaching efforts.
	Teachers disaggregate and openly discuss data in collaborative team meetings, and the outcomes guide future instruction.	Data are used as a part of planning and as a focus to help teachers' instructional practice.	Data are treated as private for fear that sharing will offend teachers. There is little, if any, data analysis taking place, and many teachers fear or distrust data.

Instruction *(continued)*	Students are active partners in their education and are given choices and input in classroom meetings.	Teachers decide on the best approach for their students according to assessment results and identified goals.	There are no expectations of student involvement in learning plans. Staff members do not offer or discuss opportunities for student input.
	Classroom observations by colleagues and administrators are regular occurrences that are followed by timely, constructive conferences and feedback to assist with professional growth.	Observations are conducted by supervisors in accordance with regulations. The required feedback may be misinterpreted at times.	Observations are conducted only when a teacher is not meeting performance objectives. The general staff consensus is that the evaluation system is ineffective.
	Instructional time is sacred and protected. Interruptions, PA announcements, assemblies, and fire drills are kept to a minimum. When they must occur, time is built into the schedule, or the schedule is adjusted accordingly.	Interruptions do occur, but they are not a regular occurrence. If staff members would work a little harder at adjusting schedules and finding a balance between periods that are affected by these interruptions, the faculty would generally believe in the importance of bell-to-bell instruction.	PA announcements are a frequent occurrence during the school day, even after the regular announcements have been made. No consideration is given to balancing interrupted class time.

	Indicators of a Healthy Culture	Indicators of a Benign Culture	Indicators of an Ill Culture
Extracurricular Life	A cross section of students is involved in clubs, activities, and sports, which are recognized as an important part of students' educational life.	Attendance of and participation in extracurricular activities are evident. There are times when the community seems to hold extracurricular life as more important than academics, but academics are also held as a high priority.	Teams are hard to fill, and there is a lack of interest in extracurricular activities. Games and after-school shows have poor attendance, and teams and events are considered unsuccessful.
	After the school day has ended, the building is still filled with vibrant life and appears to be more of a community center than a schoolhouse.	There are activities after school, but only those who would be expected to be involved attend them.	Activities exist but may not be attended by subgroups in proportion to the school's demographics. Lack of involvement is evident.
	Community members and parents are visible and are continually encouraged to visit and participate in events and activities.	There is a general understanding that parents are welcome, but there are no evident plans or programs to engage underrepresented families.	Parent participation appears to be cliquish and difficult to penetrate by newcomers.
Discipline	Classroom misbehavior is rare. Instruction engages students, and the teacher addresses inappropriate behavior in a nonconfrontational manner.	Students are generally compliant and respectful; however, the rules and consequences may differ from one teacher to another, with varied support from the administration.	Classroom misbehavior is frequent. Students are uninterested in lessons and misbehave often, provoking the teacher or being provoked by staff when the behavior is addressed.

Discipline *(continued)*	Teachers have established agreed-upon classroom routines, behavior expectations, and consequences that are clear and consistent from one class or teacher to another.	Teachers enforce their own policies. There is little, if any, sharing of strategies and best practices with other professionals in the building.	Misbehavior is rampant and unbalanced. Student and teacher personalities play a major role in discipline policy, with favorites and resentments.
	Misbehavior is primarily addressed by the classroom teacher, who keeps parents engaged and the administration and counselor notified as appropriate.	Teachers handle the majority of their own classroom discipline issues. Parents are randomly notified and not invited to contribute to the solutions, and administrators are only aware of serious infractions.	Misbehavior is rarely handled by the teacher within the classroom. Students are often removed from the class, missing excessive instructional time. There is little communication with parents until the behavior reaches crisis mode.
	Teachers are the primary disciplinarians and meet in collaborative teams to discuss discipline. Administrators act as a secondary support to classroom teachers, providing guidance for chronic or serious behavior infractions.	Veteran teachers receive (and need) minimal discipline support. Administration is expected to provide additional support to the new staff and is sometimes called on to bring order to a classroom or to troubleshoot discipline problems for teachers.	Administrators spend most of their time as classroom managers. Teachers expect administration to bring order to their classes but lose student respect because discipline disappears as soon as the administrator leaves the classroom.

	Indicators of a Healthy Culture	Indicators of a Benign Culture	Indicators of an Ill Culture
Discipline (continued)	Discipline referrals are infrequent and are seen as a last resort. Teachers implement agreed-upon schoolwide standards before processing a referral.	The frequency of discipline referrals varies. Some teachers frequently use the referral process, while others don't and perhaps should be referring some issues for administrative support.	Discipline referrals are plentiful—often excessive—and students are regularly referred for minor infractions and perceived infractions.
	Administrators quickly respond to referrals while maintaining full communication with teachers and parents.	Administrators pick and choose which referrals to address, often depending on which teacher submits the referral. Referrals addressed include feedback to teachers and students.	Administrators either ignore referrals, leading teachers to feel unsupported, or cannot address them because of the sheer numbers; only the serious referrals get the necessary attention.
	School rules are clearly communicated, consistently applied, and equally enforced by all teachers and administrators.	Although it may vary from class to class, discipline in most cases is handled effectively by teachers and administrators.	School rules are rarely enforced consistently; students are able to do things in some classes that they are not permitted to do in others.
Environment	The building is clean, orderly, and attractive, both inside and outside.	Although the interior and/or exterior of the building aren't always clean, there do not appear to be signs of neglect.	Aside from trash and litter scattered around inside and outside, the state of the bathrooms is the telltale sign here.

Environment (continued)	Visitors are welcome in the building, and the main office sets a warm, professional, and responsive tone that also indicates that safety and security are a priority.	Although visitors are welcome, nothing seems to make them feel special or particularly cared about when they are there. People generally feel safe here.	Visitors are treated with suspicion, and the main office is a place that people avoid for its unprofessional atmosphere or uninviting tone. Safety and security procedures may be nonexistent, or they may have swung too far to the other end of the spectrum.
	The school's vision and mission are posted prominently, and displays of student work, school success, and slogans and quotations are evident not just in the main office but throughout the building as well.	Although the school's vision and mission are visible in the main office and posted in prominent places in the building, other kinds of displays are outdated or nonexistent elsewhere in the school.	It is difficult to determine the school's vision and mission. Visitors can easily discern a negative climate and low morale through the lack of visible evidence that the school celebrates its students, staff, and successes.
	Teachers regularly dress professionally, especially for major events, meetings, or activities, conveying respect, pride, and a willingness to model societal expectations.	Most teachers dress professionally, but some staff members insist on wearing jeans throughout the week.	Most teachers regularly wear jeans, warm-up suits, and even flip-flops. Attempts by some staff members to dress more professionally are met with ridicule or with persuasion or coercion to dress down.

Resource

2

Survey for Leadership

The purpose of this survey is to provide objective information about your administrator, department chair, team leader, or other school leader with whom you work on a regular basis. The results will be used to review and reflect on his or her leadership style, skills, and impact, and perceptions by others. The information from this survey will be used by the leader to set goals and address areas of strength and areas that need improvement. Your accurate feedback is extremely important and will remain anonymous.

Please rate each item by indicating whether you strongly agree, agree, have no opinion, disagree, or strongly disagree. Place a check or "X" in the appropriate box by each item below. Your time is valued and greatly appreciated.

Skill	Strongly Agree	Agree	No Opinion	Disagree	Strongly Disagree
Instructional Leader					
reviews and becomes familiar with different curricula					
showcases best instructional practices					
conducts observations					
provides quality feedback from observations					
maintains a presence in classrooms					
meets with teachers and teacher teams on an ongoing basis					
ensures that you have the necessary resources to perform your job					
provides appropriate levels of monitoring					
is effective as a leader					

Skill	Strongly Agree	Agree	No Opinion	Disagree	Strongly Disagree
is a respected school leader					
values a leadership team					
Inspires and Develops					
inspires others					
develops leadership capacity in others					
is an effective mentor					
empowers others					
nurtures staff leadership skills					
provides support					
identifies and provides appropriate staff development					
celebrates victories and gains with staff					
is able to enlist followers					
shares responsibility					
respects you as a professional					
is a facilitator of others					
builds leadership capacity					
allows you to construct your own knowledge					
provides positive reinforcement					
encourages others					
shares leadership responsibilities with others					

Skill	Strongly Agree	Agree	No Opinion	Disagree	Strongly Disagree
Communication					
pinpoints problems through effective questioning					
provides a vision					
communicates well in writing					
communicates well verbally, in person					
communicates well at public gatherings or assemblies					
communicates clear expectations of staff					
communicates clear expectations of students					
is open to new ideas					
refers to you by name					
clearly communicates goals for the school					
communicates reasonable expectations					
encourages feedback from others					
articulates a clear purpose for the leadership team and other teams					
is professionally approachable					
demonstrates an ability to communicate with all types of personalities					
is personally approachable					
shares information when appropriate					
gives you specific and positive feedback					

Skill	Strongly Agree	Agree	No Opinion	Disagree	Strongly Disagree
Uses Data					
performs data analysis					
relies on data to identify areas for improvement					
identifies results to measure effectiveness					
reviews and analyzes assessment data					
Discipline					
effectively addresses low- or nonperforming staff					
enforces policies and rules					
Models					
exhibits energy and enthusiasm					
maintains a persona that others want to emulate					
demonstrates creativity					
demonstrates focus					
leads by example					
models expected behaviors of others					
demonstrates patience					
dresses appropriately					
develops and follows norms					
maintains visibility on a regular basis at events, at lunch, in halls, and in classrooms					

Skill	Strongly Agree	Agree	No Opinion	Disagree	Strongly Disagree
maintains a presence in the building					
Decisions					
makes good hiring decisions					
listens well and then makes decisions					
is a collective decision maker when appropriate					
makes appropriate adjustments when confronted with an obstacle					
makes appropriate adjustments in leadership style depending on the type of task or staff involved					
makes tough decisions					
develops and implements action plans to address issues					
follows through on promises					
follows through on initiatives					
initiates, originates, and innovates effectively					
identifies solutions to problems and tasks					
Facility Operations					
coordinates building operations					
ensures that the school operates efficiently					
conducts effective and meaningful meetings					
provides meeting schedules					

Skill	Strongly Agree	Agree	No Opinion	Disagree	Strongly Disagree
provides time for collaboration					
provides time with other school staff for vertical collaboration					
Personal Attributes					
demonstrates care and concern in words and actions					
shows empathy					
protects staff from ill effects of others (e.g., outside supervisors, parents, school board)					
takes the time to say hello and checks in at a personal level					
provides positive recognition					
does not retaliate when irritated					
thanks people publicly and privately					
forges collegial, not top-down, relationships					
maintains credibility					
owns mistakes					
is willing to do what he or she delegates to others					
has a balanced personality					
has an appropriate level of ego					
demonstrates humility when appropriate					
is aware of his or her own weaknesses					
demonstrates patience with others					

Skill	Strongly Agree	Agree	No Opinion	Disagree	Strongly Disagree
preserves an open-door policy					
demonstrates honesty					
works in fairness with all staff					
works in fairness with all students					
is well organized					
maintains a positive attitude and approach					
is student-centered					

Resource	Curriculum Review
3	

Approximate Time

Ongoing and throughout the year; quarterly or more frequently if possible.

Attendees/Participants

Leadership team members and teachers of common grade level and/or subject.

Purpose

Conduct curriculum review discussions among teachers and members of the leadership team to ensure that what should be taught is actually being taught.

Directions

1. Assemble teacher teams of common grade level and/or subject.
2. Discuss the purpose and desired outcomes of curriculum review meetings.
3. Share research that explains and supports the concept of curriculum reviews.
4. Develop a format to facilitate discussions (see curriculum review form, p. 222). Use the questions to start the conversation and solicit input from the team to identify other important information to discuss at curriculum reviews.
5. Schedule future meetings.
6. Distribute or post the curriculum review form for easy access prior to each meeting. Each member is expected to bring at least one completed example for the curriculum review discussion. Teachers should bring enough copies for each team member to have one.
7. Divide the number of meeting minutes by the number of members in the meeting. For example, a one-hour meeting with six members will provide 10 minutes for each member.
8. Divide each member's allotted time by two to provide a period for sharing and presenting and a period for questions and answers. Ensure that the process provides time for each member to participate.
9. Organize a notebook to maintain a record of the meeting dates and attendance, member participation, and content reviews. Share the record with the leadership team.
10. Record curriculum information on the curriculum information sheet (see p. 223).

Follow-Up

Near the end of the year, assemble the team and review the completed curriculum information sheet. Consider any adjustments for the following year, including additions, cuts, and revisions. This form is an invaluable tool that will provide support to new membership (especially new teachers) and objective information for continuous improvement efforts.

Materials

- Curriculum review form.
- Curriculum review research.
- Sample lessons (provided by teachers).
- Sample assessments (provided by teachers).
- Sample projects (provided by teachers).
- Copies of standards (provided by state or school system).
- Notebooks.

Curriculum Review Form

Name _____   Date _____

Subject/Team _____   Lesson/Unit _____

How did your students fare on this assignment?	*Above Expectation*	*At Expectation*	*Below Expectation*
Why do you think that is?			
How do you think the delivery and reception of this lesson or unit went?			
Describe the format of the lesson.			
Explain activities used.			

How did your students fare on this assignment?	*Above Expectation*	*At Expectation*	*Below Expectation*
What standards or objectives were covered?			
Identify types of assessments used to measure effectiveness.			
Did students develop projects as an outcome? If so, please share a sample.			
Identify desired modifications for future applications.			

Curriculum Information Sheet

Month	Subject and Objectives	Evidence of Lesson, Examples, Activities
SEPT.		
OCT.		
NOV.		

Month	Subject and Objectives	Evidence of Lesson, Examples, Activities
DEC.		
JAN.		
FEB.		
MAR.		
APR.		
MAY		
JUNE		

Resource

4

Work Plan Memorandum

Approximate Time

Varied.

Attendees/Participants

Administrator and receiving staff member.

Purpose

Maintain mutual accountability for all staff and enforce compliance when necessary.

Directions

1. Have a discussion with the staff member who has not been arriving on time. Hopefully, you can resolve the issue immediately, and written documentation will not be necessary.
2. If the discussion leads you to believe that the staff member will not be able to rectify the issue alone or is blatantly refusing to comply, then discuss the details of the work plan memorandum. Be specific about due dates, expected behavior from this discussion forward, and possible consequences for noncompliance. Follow up the discussion in writing to avoid misunderstandings.
3. Deliver the completed work plan memorandum within 24 hours.

Follow-Up

Recognize your staff member for improvement and continue with documentation if the behavior has not been not corrected. If the behavior continues, contact human resources to place the staff member on an evaluation cycle or to confirm that you will take appropriate measures for nonrenewal of contract. If the staff member's inappropriate behavior continues, you may need to move forward with the appropriate process for nonrenewal of contract.

Materials

- Work plan memorandum.
- Additional documentation as evidence of a pattern of behavior.

Sample Work Plan Memorandum

DATE:

TO: *[Name of noncompliant staff member]*, *[Title]*

FROM: *[Your name]*, *[Title]*

SUBJECT: Work Plan

The purpose of this memorandum is to confirm our discussion on *[date]* on your arrival time to work. I expressed my confidence in your ability to rectify the pattern of behavior; you explained that you would try but were not sure you could consistently arrive to work on time due to several reasons. Out of fairness and professional respect to you, I will offer assistance while holding you to the same standards of accountability as other staff in this school.

To clarify my position on this issue, you are expected to be at work on time each day. On *[date—usually a week from delivery of this memorandum]* please submit a work plan outlining the steps you will take to improve your attendance. Starting on *[date—usually the same date the plan is due]*, I am requesting that you sign in each morning in my office when you arrive to work. If you are consistently on time each day for one month, you will not be required to continue this sign-in procedure.

I hope this will encourage you to arrive on time each day. If your tardiness continues, it may result in disciplinary action. I look forward to seeing your work plan and a resolution to this issue. As you know, it is important for all members of the leadership team to hold and demonstrate high personal and professional standards. If you have any questions regarding this memorandum, please feel free to see me.

cc: Local Site File

Resource	
5	**Vision Development Worksheet**

Approximate Time

One or more meetings; don't rush the process.

Attendees/Participants

Vision oversight committee representing all areas of the school. Each representative acts as a liaison between his or her respective team or department and the leadership team members.

Purpose

Develop a collectively created vision statement.

Directions

1. Identify and assemble the vision oversight committee.
2. Discuss the expected outcome of the committee and provide clear guidelines, timelines, the school's current vision statement, examples of other vision statements, and pertinent articles about vision statements.
3. After committee members have time to review the clarifying questions in Chapter 2, provide a copy of the vision development worksheet (see p. 228).
4. Ask the committee members to use key words from the articles and their professional judgment to answer the questions on the worksheet, listing words or phrases on sticky notes (one idea per sticky note).
5. Place eight sheets of poster paper around the room and write one prompt at the top of each sheet. Ask each committee member to place his or her sticky notes on the corresponding sheets.
6. Provide time for each member to see all the responses on each sheet.
7. After reviewing the responses, the committee will discuss which responses are "absolutes" to the vision statement and move them to the top of the sheet; those that the committee agrees are less critical will get moved toward the bottom of the sheet.
8. Ask one or two committee members to gather all the "absolutes" and start assembling a vision statement based on the direction and input they receive from the rest of the group.
9. Once the committee members reach agreement on a vision statement, they should share it with the entire staff for feedback and critiques.
10. Feedback and critiques are brought back to the vision oversight committee for review and revision if necessary.

Follow-Up

Recognize the vision oversight committee members for their efforts and accomplishment. Share the vision statement with staff, students, and parents. Challenge school functions that are not supportive of the vision statement. Post the vision statement in public, visible places.

Materials

- Vision development worksheet.
- Examples of vision statements, including a copy of the school's current vision statement.
- Sticky notes, poster paper.

Vision Development Worksheet

In your group, using key words from the articles and your professional judgment, answer the following questions by listing single words or phrases on sticky notes (one idea per sticky note). Take this sheet with you to each sheet of poster paper and place your sticky notes on the corresponding sheets.

What would you like to see your school become, for its own sake?	(sticky note)	What reputation would it have?	(sticky note)
What kinds of learning experiences would it provide?	(sticky note)	What contribution would it make?	(sticky note)

What do your school and its teachers value?	(sticky note)	How would people work together?	(sticky note)
What do your school and its teachers believe?	(sticky note)	How would people handle good and bad times?	(sticky note)

Resource

6

Mission Development Worksheet

Approximate Time

One or more meetings; don't rush the process.

Attendees/Participants

Mission oversight committee representing all areas of the school. Each representative acts as a liaison between his or her respective team or department and the leadership team members.

Purpose

Develop a mission statement that reflects and supports the new vision statement.

Directions

1. Identify and assemble the mission oversight committee.
2. Discuss the expected outcome of the committee and provide clear guidelines, timelines, the school's current mission statement, and examples of other mission statements.
3. After committee members have time to review the new vision statement, provide a copy of the mission development worksheet (see p. 231).
4. Ask the committee members to use key words from the sample statements and their professional judgment to answer the questions on the worksheet, listing words or phrases on sticky notes (one idea per sticky note).
5. Place four sheets of poster paper around the room and write one prompt at the top of each sheet. Ask each committee member to place his or her sticky notes on the corresponding sheets.
6. Provide time for each member to see all the responses on each sheet.
7. After reviewing the responses, the committee will discuss which responses are "absolutes" to the mission statement and move them to the top of the sheet; those that the committee agrees are less critical will get moved toward the bottom of the sheet.
8. Ask one or two of the members to gather all the "absolutes" and start assembling a mission statement using the sticky notes based on the direction and input they receive from the rest of the group.
9. Once the committee members reach agreement on a new mission statement, they should share it with the entire staff for feedback and critiques.
10. Feedback and critiques are brought back to the mission oversight committee for review and revision if necessary.

Follow-Up

Recognize the mission oversight committee members for their efforts and accomplishment. Share the vision and mission statements with staff, students, and parents. Continue to challenge school functions that are not supportive of the vision and mission statements. Post both statements in public, visible places.

Materials

- Mission development worksheet.
- The school's new vision statement, the school's current mission statement, and examples of other mission statements.
- Sticky notes, poster paper.

Mission Development Worksheet

Review the current mission statement and the new vision statement. Write your responses to the following prompts by listing single words or phrases on sticky notes (one idea per sticky note).

Take this sheet with you to each sheet of poster paper and place your sticky notes on the corresponding sheets.

How do you envision your school becoming what you hope it to be?	(sticky note)
What processes might it conduct?	(sticky note)

How would people work together, and what would they do when they gather?	(sticky note)
What are the necessary steps you would need to take?	(sticky note)

Resource

7

Best Lesson Worksheet

Approximate Time

30 minutes or longer, depending on group size.

Attendees/Participants

Variable; this resource can be used by staff members meeting from the same team, department, or school or from more than one team, department, or school.

Purpose

Facilitate focused discussions on best lessons among staff members.

Directions

1. Assemble staff at tables, with no more than six people at each table.
2. While distributing the best lesson worksheet (see p. 234), explain the purpose of this activity and identify its intended outcomes. You may want to explain the value of sharing best lessons with one another and ask participants where and how they learned their best lessons. This will get them thinking about best lessons. If staff members seem unsure about what constitutes a best lesson, ask them to recall a best lesson that they remember as a student.
3. Ask participants to independently fill in the column on the right side of the table without discussing their responses. If you think staff members will be lost with this activity, use an overhead projector to display a copy of the form with sample information in the blank column. Once everyone at a table has completed the form, let them talk about their findings until the rest of the group has completed the task.
4. Regroup the staff into small teams of three (if possible, grouping people who do not typically work together).
5. Ask each member of each triad to take one minute to share his or her responses, giving the other two members one minute to comment and ask clarifying questions.
6. Ask each triad to identify one practice to share with the rest of the meeting participants. Depending on the size of the group, you can pick the triads to share the practice they agreed to share with others.

Follow-Up

Collect the forms, and review them with the leadership team to determine potential lesson demonstrations and proposals for future presentations. Another way to keep this moving is to ask team leaders or department chairs to continue the discussions about best lessons at team or department meetings. You might also have your leaders encourage their teachers to share highlights from their triad discussions that the team or department could consider adopting as its own practices.

Materials

- Best lesson worksheet.
- Writing utensil for each participant.

Best Lesson Worksheet

Name _____ Group/Team _____

Your School _____ Date _____

Subject/Topic/Explanation	
Why was it one of the best?	
What was the format?	
How were students engaged?	

Was there an evaluation? If so, what type?	
Where did you get the lesson idea?	
Have you shared this lesson with others?	
Could you demonstrate this lesson for the faculty?	

Resource

8

Peer Observation Feedback Form

Approximate Time

Five minutes or longer to complete the form, plus a 10-minute introduction to staff before implementation.

Attendees/Participants

Teachers who are observing colleagues. The completed form will be received by the observed teacher and the supervising administrator.

Purpose

Provide positive feedback to the observed teacher; gain schoolwide knowledge of strategies, models, and quality practices in classrooms throughout the building; and provide necessary documentation for administrative support to address notable events or a lack of participation in the peer observation process.

Directions

1. Explain the process and expectations for peer observations.
2. Share the form that will be used with the staff.
3. Provide time for staff to discuss their concerns and share potential positive outcomes. Ask the staff for suggestions to resolve any concerns and highlight the possible positive outcomes.
4. Ask staff to fill out the form during the observation, recording nothing negative.
5. Ask the observer to make a copy of the completed form and submit one copy to the observed teacher and the other to the supervising administrator.

Follow-Up

1. Log the peer observation feedback forms to monitor who has been observed and who has completed an observation within the participation time frame. Follow up with those who have not participated.
2. Identify a date to review and revise the form to fit the specific needs of your school and staff.

Materials

- Peer observation feedback form.
- Timeline to complete observations.
- Schedule for peer observations.

Sample Peer Observation Feedback Form

Date: _____

Dear _____,

Thank you for the opportunity to observe your class. I really enjoyed the visit on
_____*[date]*_____ during ___*[period or hour]*___. Although several practices
were intriguing, the one that I think I will attempt in my class is

_____

_____

_____

_____.

It is nice to know when implementing something new that you have a resource in
the building who has experience with the model. I look forward to talking with you
soon about my experience with implementation.

Sincerely,

_____*[Name]*_____

cc: Supervising Administrator

Resource

9

Peer Observation Memorandum

Approximate Time

Varied.

Attendees/Participants

Administrator and receiving staff member.

Purpose

Support a peer observation model with consistent expectations of all staff. This memorandum will also serve as documentation for an evaluation or contract renewal consideration if the staff member does not change the behavior.

Directions

1. Have a discussion with the staff member who has not been participating in peer observations, and remind him or her when the expectations were discussed with all staff. Ask the staff member to identify when he or she will complete the observation.

2. Follow up on or shortly after the staff member's commitment date; either thank the staff member for the follow-through or explain your disappointment with the lack of follow-up and insist that he or she identify another date for completion in the near future.

3. Follow up again on or after the second identified date. If the staff member has not fulfilled his or her responsibility, assign a date as a deadline. Explain that you will document this discussion, and send him or her a memo with the details. Also inform the staff member that his or her immediate response to this directive is expected and will prevent possible disciplinary action.

4. Deliver the completed peer observation memorandum within 24 hours.

Follow-Up

On or shortly after the assigned observation date, check to see whether the staff member has complied with the directive. If not, cite him or her for insubordination with a copy to the local file and to human resources (you may want to contact human resources to make sure you are in compliance with their insubordination guidelines). If this or similar behavior continues, move forward with evaluation documentation and, possibly, take appropriate measures for nonrenewal of contract.

Materials

- Peer observation memorandum.
- Additional documentation as evidence of a pattern of behavior.

Sample Peer Observation Memorandum

DATE:

TO: *[Name], [Title]*

FROM: *[Your Name], [Title]*

SUBJECT: Peer Observations

The purpose of this memorandum is to confirm our discussion on *[date]* on peer observation expectations. I reminded you that you were first informed during the inservice days at the beginning of the school year that all teachers were expected to conduct at least one peer observation with feedback during the first nine weeks of school. On *[date of first discussion about not submitting peer observation feedback]*, we discussed that you had not submitted evidence of your peer observation. You said that you had been very busy and just did not have the time but that you would work on fulfilling that obligation in the near future. We spoke again about the same issue on *[date of next discussion]* and *[date of follow-up discussion]*. On both occasions, you said you were going to schedule and conduct an observation soon.

Yesterday, I explained that I am now assigning you a deadline of *[date—usually within one month of this memorandum]* to complete this task. In the future, you are expected to meet your obligations within the given timelines without reminders. If you do not comply with this directive, your lack of action will be considered insubordination and may be followed up with administrative consequences that could eventually lead to a recommendation for termination.

Your prompt attention to this memo is greatly appreciated. I look forward to seeing your peer observation feedback.

cc: Supervising Administrator

School File

Resource

10

Best Practices Worksheet

Approximate Time

45 minutes or longer, depending on group size.

Attendees/Participants

Variable; this resource can be used by staff members meeting from the same team, department, or school or from more than one team, department, or school.

Purpose

Facilitate focused discussions on best practices among staff members. The outcomes are not curriculum-specific but are observable behaviors (e.g., starting class, ending class, interruptions, makeup work, hall passes, use of technology, transitions, grouping, and so on).

Directions

1. Assemble staff at tables, with no more than six people at each table.
2. While distributing the best practices worksheet, explain the purpose of this activity and identify its intended outcomes. You may want to explain the value of sharing best practices with one another and ask participants where and how they learned their best practices. This will help get them thinking about their practices. If staff members seem unsure about what constitute best practices, ask them to think about a notable practice they observed or heard about and have been considering using in their own class.
3. Ask participants to independently fill in two or three rows with some of their best practices and to place an "X" in the appropriate column on the right. Provide a few minutes for discussion.
4. Group the teachers by grade level, department, or team and have them share their practices with their groups. While one is sharing, the others should be recording the practices in the additional blank rows on their forms.
5. Have the groups discuss each practice, identify one or more that they could try in their classrooms, and share their selection with the staff.

Follow-Up

Ask leadership team members to conduct follow-up discussions with their departments or teams, and ask each to bring a best practice back to the next leadership team meeting for schoolwide implementation. Ensure that communication is occurring vertically in the hierarchy.

Materials

- Best practices worksheet.
- Writing utensil for each participant.
- Whiteboard, overhead projector, or LCD projector for presenting.

Best Practices Worksheet

Name _____ Group/Team _____

Your School _____ Date _____

Observable Activities Use this space to list activities, instructional practices, or other observable behaviors that might be good for other classrooms or learning environments.	Other	Instruction	Management	First 5 Minutes	Any 20 Minutes	Last 5 Minutes

Resource 11

Walk-Through Expectations

Approximate Time

Ongoing throughout the year.

Attendees/Participants

Teachers, support staff, and administrators.

Purpose

Provide consistent expectations and "look-for's" when conducting walk-through observations.

Directions

1. During a leadership team meeting, distribute and discuss the walk-through expectations form. Allow a couple of minutes for open discussion about the contents, then explain the purpose of using this form.
2. Review the items with your team and decide what should be kept and what should be removed.
3. With your team's assistance, create a manageable form for walk-through observations.
4. Before rolling the form out to others in the school, ask leadership team members to field-test it by observing one another.
5. After each member has used the form, reconvene the leadership team and ask for suggestions to improve the form for ease of use.
6. Make a final draft of the form and share it with the staff before it is used.
7. You may want to solicit input from all staff before implementation.

Follow-Up

1. Identify a date to make edits and revisions.
2. Continue to look for ways to make the form user-friendly.
3. Include your leadership team in discussions about adding or deleting content from the form to keep it current and applicable to the school's needs.

Materials

- Walk-through expectations form.

Walk-Through Expectations Form

Observed	Notable	Needs Improvement	Observable Behaviors	Additional Notes
Planning and Assessment				
			Teacher delivers accurate instructional content.	
			Students explain their answers and conclusions.	
			Teacher demonstrates appropriate wait time.	
			Teacher uses formative assessments.	
			Assessment formats align with those of high-stakes tests.	
			Teacher uses varied assessment methods.	
			Teacher provides meaningful feedback to students.	
			Teacher calls on a variety of students.	
			Teacher checks for understanding.	
			Teacher makes lesson adjustments on the basis of student interaction.	

Observed	Notable	Needs Improvement	Observable Behaviors	Additional Notes
Instruction				
			Instruction includes warm-up: review, practice, or preview of the day's material.	
			Instruction is aligned with school system and state curriculum.	
			The lesson is focused on objective(s).	
			The lesson maintains instructional focus.	
			The difficulty of questions varies.	
			Lesson maximizes learning time.	
			Teacher uses differentiated instruction.	
			Lesson includes guided and independent practice.	
			Teacher uses direct instruction with the whole class.	
			Teacher uses direct instruction with small groups.	
			Instruction integrates cooperative learning.	
			Instruction includes closure.	

Observed	Notable	Needs Improvement	Observable Behaviors	Additional Notes
Learning Environment				
			Teacher efficiently manages routine responsibilities.	
			Teacher takes attendance during first five minutes of class.	
			Teacher engages students at beginning of class.	
			Teacher engages students at end of class.	
			Teacher puts classroom procedures in place.	
			Behavioral expectations and rules are clear.	
			Teacher effectively handles routines and transitions.	
			Teacher provides a safe, orderly, and organized learning environment.	
			Students are actively engaged throughout the period.	
			The lesson integrates technology.	

Observed	Notable	Needs Improvement	Observable Behaviors	Additional Notes
Communication				
			Teacher communicates lesson objective.	
			Teacher communicates agenda.	
			Teacher gives concise instructional directions.	
			Teacher displays student work.	
			Teacher greets students at the door.	
			Teacher is enthusiastic and sets a positive tone.	
			Teacher provides a positive atmosphere and positive reinforcement.	
			Teacher and students convey mutual respect.	
			Teacher uses students' names.	

Observed	Notable	Needs Improvement	Team-Teaching Expectations and Observable Behaviors	Additional Notes
Planning and Assessment				
			Teachers have written lesson plans.	
			Assessment design • Teachers make accommodations prior to assessment. • Any student needing remediation receives access to modified assessments.	
			One person grades all assessments for that specific assessment tool. (Teachers may alternate grading responsibilities accordingly.)	
			Teachers use one specific grading rubric.	
			Both teachers identify and communicate specific student performance expectations.	

Observed	Notable	Needs Improvement	Team-Teaching Expectations and Observable Behaviors	Additional Notes
Instruction				
			Teachers establish instructional routines.	
			Teachers assign instructional duties on a daily, weekly, or monthly basis or by specific units of study.	
			One teacher delivers instruction while the other monitors student on-task behaviors, answers student questions, and provides clarification.	
			Within the class period, both teachers should deliver direct instruction.	
			Warm-up.	
			Main body of instruction.	
			Homework.	
			Summary and wrap-up.	
			Modeling (e.g., one teacher introduces a strategy, after which both teachers model the strategy and check for student understanding).	

Observed	Notable	Needs Improvement	Team-Teaching Expectations and Observable Behaviors	Additional Notes
Instruction *(continued)*				
			Teachers ensure that all students have recorded their upcoming assignments and projects.	
Learning Environment				
			Teachers monitor student behavior and maintain momentum of instruction.	
			Teachers plan student behavior expectations.	
			Teachers develop specific behavior consequences.	
Communication				
			Both teachers should be familiar with all students' progress or lack of progress and be able to articulate information to parent/guardian, counselor, or administrator.	
			General education and special education teachers are jointly responsible for	
			Instruction.	
			Planning.	
			Behavior management.	
			Grading.	
			Conferences.	

Observed	Notable	Needs Improvement	Team-Teaching Expectations and Observable Behaviors	Additional Notes
Communication *(continued)*				
			Evidence of a variety of instructional arrangements.	
			Both teachers are responsible for creating and maintaining a positive classroom climate that includes	
			Students listening and responding to both teachers.	
			Students asking for assistance from both teachers.	
			Both teachers conferencing, grading, and giving assignments.	
			Both teachers redirecting students and managing class.	

Resource 12

Class Evaluation Survey

Just as teachers want to have a voice in how their school is run, students feel the same about their classes. Some teachers are afraid to seek student input and feedback because they fear relinquishing control, but holding class meetings with each period is one way to foster and build community. Giving students a voice can oftentimes improve motivation, morale, and climate.

Administer a survey that students fill out anonymously a few times during the year to assess how they feel about their progress, the class, and the like; then follow up with them by sharing and discussing the results. You might prefer using a Likert scale instead of short response questions, but either format will yield important information.

1. How has the pace of instruction been so far?
2. Can you list three essential items that you have learned?
3. What type of instruction has appealed to you the most (group work, independent work, class discussion, overhead instruction, PowerPoint presentations, etc.) and why?
4. Have I been approachable and responsive to your needs? Why or why not?
5. Have I been available when you needed me?
6. Do you think that you need extra help? If so, what kind? In which areas?
7. Are you happy with your present grade?
8. If not, what three things do you plan to do to improve it?
9. Do you have a favorite class session? A least favorite class session?
10. What do you enjoy most about class? Least about class?
11. How confident do you feel in your ability to succeed in this class?
12. Do you believe that your grades have been fair and lacking bias?
13. Do you think that your study skills have improved this year? If so, in what areas? Where do you still need to improve?
14. What from the first semester/quarter are you most proud of?
15. What from the first semester/quarter are you least proud of?
16. What goals do you have for this new quarter/semester? What steps will you take to achieve them?
17. If you achieved your first semester goals, how did you do so?
18. What advice, suggestions, and words of wisdom would you give to future students taking this class?
19. What suggestions do you have to improve class?
20. General comments?

Resource 13

Good Credit Rewards Program

Good Credit Rewards Qualifications				
	Platinum	*Gold*	*Silver*	*Application Pending*
Grade level eligibility	11–12	All grades	All grades	All grades
Attendance				
Absences each quarter	1 or fewer	3 or fewer	5 or fewer	Assessing status
Unexcused absences each quarter	0	1	1	Assessing status
Class skips	0	1	1	Assessing status
Tardies	3 or fewer	5 or fewer	7 or fewer	Assessing status
Discipline				
Discipline referrals	0 (admin. discretion)	3 or fewer (admin. discretion)	5 or fewer (admin. discretion)	Assessing status
Grades				
Last quarter's grades	3.25 GPA or higher	2.5 GPA or higher	No more than 1 *F*	Assessing status
Cumulative GPA	3.25 GPA or higher	2.5 GPA or higher	2.0 GPA or higher	Assessing status

Good Credit Rewards Privileges			
	Platinum	*Gold*	*Silver*
Extracurricular and Community Functions			
Athletic events	Free access to events	5% discount to events	Regular price
Community	10% discount at participating merchants	5% discount at participating merchants	No discounts available
Extracurricular activities	Eligible to participate in all extracurricular activities		
Cookout	Free cookout each semester (Ask local merchants to contribute prizes and giveaways.)		Not eligible
School trips	End-of-year activities (e.g., amusements, bowling, games, hiking, park trip)		Not eligible
Attendance			
Hall passes	No hall pass necessary	Standard hall pass required	
End of quarter	Early dismissal on last day (teacher discretion)		Not eligible
End of semester	Exemption from final exams		Not eligible
Lunch	Early dismissal for lunch (teacher discretion)	Not eligible	Not eligible
Miscellaneous			
Parking spaces	Reserved row of parking spaces closest to the school		Not eligible
Special incentives	(Depending on your school, community, and parental involvement, many suggestions could be entertained. Brainstorm ideas from staff, students, and parents.)		Not eligible

Resource

14

Detention Slip

Approximate Time

Five minutes, plus parent/guardian contact.

Attendees/Participants

Staff members who assign detention and students who are assigned detention.

Purpose

Obligate students to take advantage of learning opportunities in place of disciplinary detentions.

Directions

1. Before implementing this program, explain to staff that the students who most commonly receive detentions are also the students in greatest need of additional academic support. These students need a nudge to take more responsibility in finding and using available resources in the school. Express how important it is for all teachers to support the effort to help students learn and improve.
2. The staff member assigning detention explains to the student that he or she can cut his or her detention in half by trading the time for academic support in the area in which the student is least successful (preferably a core academic area).
3. The assigner ensures that the student understands that his or her time must be documented by a staff member and returned to the assigner before the detention date, or the student must serve the detention as assigned.
4. The assigner fills out the first two rows, signs the administrator line, contacts a parent/guardian to explain the process, and documents the contact.
5. The student signs the form, and a copy is made. One copy is kept as a record, and the student carries one to document the detention.
6. The student completes the information in the detention exchange rows and obtains teacher signatures to validate the time served.
7. A student can serve the assigned time with more than one teacher, but the validating staff must be providing academic support to the student.

Follow-Up

Create a follow-up file for these detentions; put the student names in your calendar to check on their progress before the actual detention date. The idea is not to make sure they serve their detention but to ensure that they are learning to become academically successful by using available resources.

Materials

- Detention slip.

Detention Slip

Detention Assignment					
Student Name		Grade	Amount of Time	Hr.	Min.
Date of Notice		Date of Detention			
Opportunity to Exchange Time (Two Hours of Detention for One Hour of Support)					
Teacher Name	Date	Hours - Minutes		Teacher Signature	
Total	Hr.	Min.			

Administrator _____   Student Signature _____

Parent Contact Date _____   Time of Contact _____

Resource

15

Master Schedule

Approximate Time

Ongoing throughout the year. Master schedule discussions should start at the beginning of each academic year, and building the master schedule should start in January.

Attendees/Participants

Leadership team, master schedule builder, and aspiring master schedule builders.

Purpose

Develop a master schedule to provide time during the day for teachers of the same subject or grade level to plan and collaborate.

Directions

1. Assemble the leadership team, including the person or persons responsible for building the master schedule.
2. Share the desired outcome with all attendees. Discuss how the increasing demands on teachers warrant the need for teachers of like subjects or grade-level responsibilities to have time for professional collaboration.
3. Inform staff of a potential change in the master schedule in the following year. If possible, you should do this at the beginning of the year.
4. Schedule a full-day inservice or several meeting times close together in October or November for the scheduling team to share and discuss models of school schedules that provide time for teachers to collaborate during the day.
5. Engage team members in brainstorming and have them solicit colleagues for ideas and proven strategies to build in collaboration time for teachers.
6. Chart the responses and focus on the most feasible approaches, but do not settle for the status quo.
7. The master schedule builder takes the ideas, drafts a master schedule framework, and brings it back to the team for professional critiquing. Once team members reach agreement, share the new master schedule concept with all staff.
8. Start building the actual master schedule no later than January.
9. Assemble team members and discuss a time to pilot the new schedule before the year ends, preferably after the high-stakes testing season but early enough that the team is able to resolve conflicts before the beginning of the following school year.

Follow-Up

Once the new master schedule is finished, celebrate the team's efforts and accomplishment. As difficult as this process may have been, it is the mechanical part; the next hurdle is to get the most out of the meeting times. Reexamine the master schedule each year to ensure that it is still meeting the needs of students and staff.

Materials

- Sample master schedule.
- Sample schedules and research on alternative and creative schedules to provide time for teacher collaboration.

Sample Master Schedule

Teacher Name	Subject	1st	Crs	2nd	Crs	3rd	Crs	4th	Crs	5th	Crs	6th	Crs	7th	Crs
ACES															
Teacher 1	English 7th	28	GTSB	12	E S	28	E	28	E	28	E		Collab	Team	
Teacher 2	English 7th			15	E			15	E				Collab	Team	
Teacher 3	English Special ED			10	E LD	28	GTSB	10	E LD				Collab	Team	
Teacher 4	History 7th	28	H	28	H				Collab	12	H S	28	H	Team	
Teacher 5	History 7th								Collab	15	H	15	H	Team	
Teacher 6	History 7th Special ED								Collab	10	H LD	10	H LD	Team	
Teacher 7	Math 7th	28	M	28	M			12	M S	28	M	28	M H	Team	
Teacher 8	Math 7th			28	M			15	M					Team	
Teacher 9	Math 7th Special ED						Collab	10	M LD					Team	
Teacher 10	Science 7th	12	S S		Collab	28	S	28	S	28	S	28	S	Team	
Teacher 11	Science 7th	15	S		Collab					15	S			Team	
Vacancy LD Science	Science 7th Special ED	10	S LD		Collab					10	S LD			Team	
ACES Subtotal		121	0	121	0	84	0	118	0	146	0	109	0	0	0

Sample Master Schedule (continued)

Teacher Name	Subject	1st	Crs	2nd	Crs	3rd	Crs	4th	Crs	5th	Crs	6th	Crs	7th	Crs
EXPLORERS															
Teacher 13	English 7th	28	E	28	GTSB	28	E	IPP	IPP	12	E S	Team	Team	28	E
Teacher 14	English 7th	28	E	28			IPP			15	E	Team	Team		
Teacher 15	English 7th LD						IPP			10	E	Team	Team		
Teacher 16	History 7th	28	H	12	H S	28	GTSB	28	Collab	28	H	Team	Team	28	H
Teacher 17	History 7th	28	H	15	H				Collab			Team	Team	28	H
Teacher 18	History 7th LD			10	H LD		IPP		Collab			Team	Team		
Teacher 19	Math 7th	12	M S	28	M		Collab	28	M H	28	M	Team	Team	28	M
Teacher 20	Math 7th	15	M				Collab					Team	Team	28	M
Teacher 21	Math 7th LD	10	M LD				Collab					Team	Team		
Teacher 22	Science 7th	28	S		Collab	28	S	12	S S	28	S	Team	Team	28	S
Teacher 23	Science 7th				Collab		IPP	15	S			28	S		
Vacancy LD Science	Science 7th LD				Collab		IPP	10	S LD			Team	Team		
EXPLORERS SUB		177	0	93	0	84	0	65	0	121	0	28	0	168	0
All subjects and classes are tallied below															
School Totals		966		913		928		910		976		926		948	

Legend

Aces and Explorers: Names of teacher teams.

Collab: Period dedicated to collaboration for the department.

E: English.

E LD: English (students with learning disabilities).

E S: English (smaller class size).

GTSB: Gifted and talented school-based program.

H: History.

H LD: History (students with learning disabilities).

H S: History (smaller class size).

IPR: Individual planning period.

M: Mathematics.

M LD: Mathematics (students with learning disabilities).

M S: Mathematics (smaller class size).

S: Science.

S LD: Science (students with learning disabilities).

S S: Science (smaller class size).

Team: This is the period dedicated for all of the teachers of that team to have common planning time.

The numbers in the period columns (1st, 2nd, 3rd, 4th, 5th, 6th, and 7th) indicate the number of seats available during that period for that class.

Resource

16

What's Our Purpose?

Approximate Time

30 minutes or longer, depending on group size.

Attendees/Participants

Attendees of ongoing professional meetings.

Purpose

Reach agreement on the purpose of teachers gathering for professional meetings.

Directions

1. This activity can be conducted within teams or departments or during an all-staff meeting.
2. Explain the purpose of the activity, including the intended outcome. This may be an activity for the shared leadership team to conduct before expanding it to other staff members, teams, and departments.
3. Each team member independently drafts a purpose statement in the first row of the table on page 263; doing so independently and without discussion is crucial to this exercise. Ask them to answer the question, What do you believe is the primary purpose of your team or departmental meetings?
4. Ask staff to form groups of five or fewer people from the same team or department; departments with fewer than five members should meet in smaller groups.
5. Each member takes one minute to share his or her draft purpose while the other members listen and take notes in the blank rows on their form.
6. Provide one minute for team members to ask the presenter clarifying questions.
7. Repeat steps 5 and 6 until all members have shared their statements.
8. Allow 10 minutes for members to review and identify essential components of the purpose statements, then draft a purpose statement that each team member supports.
9. For teams or departments with more than five members, combine the small groups and their individual drafts and then redraft a shared purpose for the department.

Follow-Up

Once a team or department has developed a purpose statement, all its meeting and agenda contents should fall under the umbrella of that purpose. If they don't, the team should redefine its purpose or critique the content of its meetings.

The purpose can also help guide leadership when teams are not functioning well. This provides clarity to what the team has agreed on when they meet.

Materials

- What's Our Purpose? form.
- Writing utensil for each participant.

What's Our Purpose?

Team or Department _____

1.
2.
3.
4.
5.
Combined agreed-upon purpose draft:

Resource 17

Meeting Norms

Approximate Time

30 minutes for creating the first draft, ongoing use at each meeting.

Attendees/Participants

Team members who have been through the forming and storming stages of group development.

Purpose

Develop meeting norms for the purpose of conducting efficient and effective meetings.

Directions

1. Assemble the team members.
2. Discuss the current state of the group's dynamics, and introduce the concept of developing meeting norms while sharing the goal and anticipated outcomes. Set a goal of identifying 5 to 10 norms from a prioritized list.
3. Distribute the meeting norms questions (see p. 265), and ask attendees to be prepared to discuss their answers and suggestions at the next meeting.
4. At the next meeting, distribute the list of norm examples (see p. 266), and explain that these are examples of norms developed by a team to protect the integrity of its meetings and that because they were developed by that team, they are more useful and valued than an adopted list.
5. After facilitating a discussion about team members' responses to the questions, ask them to identify their top five rules to include in the first draft of their meeting norms.
6. Record their choices and assign a number to each item. Again, explain that the goal is to identify no more than 5 to 10 norms.
7. Distribute sticky notes to the attendees and ask each one to write down the numbers of his or her top three to five meeting norms, one per sticky note. Then ask attendees to place their sticky notes by the corresponding items. This will provide a quick visual of a prioritized list of norms.
8. Review the results with the team members, and confirm a list of meeting norms.
9. Identify a date for review and revision. Document the list, distribute it to each member, and continue to practice the norms until they are embedded and lived by all members.

Follow-Up

We suggest doing this activity with the leadership team before having each team leader or department chair conduct it. The leadership team should set a deadline for each team to submit its norms. Revisit the process at least once a year, and make sure to celebrate this institutional cultural change.

Materials

- Meeting norms questions.

Meeting Norms Questions

Meeting Logistics • Times? • Locations? • Duration? • Frequency? • Facilitator/Chair?	
Attendance • Process for absenteeism.	
Promptness • What will our promptness policy be?	
Equal Opportunity to Participate • How can we share the workload? • Are there requirements for participation?	
Assignments • What will we expect from members? • How will actionable items from one meeting follow to the next?	
Decisions • How will decisions be agreed upon? • How will we set priorities?	

Confidentiality • How will we know what is confidential? • How will breaches of confidentiality be addressed and reconciled?	
Meeting Evaluation • How will we review our work together?	
Meeting Mechanics • Agenda. • Minutes/Notes. • Meeting Record Form.	
Courtesy • How will we encourage listening? • How will we discourage interrupting? • How can we promote respect and empathy?	
Following the Norms • How do we handle violations to our norms? • When should the norms be reviewed?	

Norm Examples

These norms were developed by a central office team:

- Meetings will start and end on time.
- Meetings will be held every Friday from 8:00 to 10:00 a.m.
- Maximum time for meetings will be two hours, with a target of one hour.
- Notes will be captured and posted before the next meeting.
- Note-taking responsibility will rotate through the team membership.
- Each member is responsible for reading the last meeting's notes before the next meeting.
- Members will bring any edits to meeting notes to the next meeting.

- Members will be notified of any meeting cancellations by e-mail before noon on Wednesday.
- Each meeting will have an agenda.
- The agenda format will include an attendance list, future note-taking responsibilities and dates, and action items that resulted from the previous meeting.
- If a member cannot take the notes on his or her assigned date, it is his or her responsibility to trade dates with another member.
- All members are expected to attend all meetings.
- Each member will identify a partner in the event of an absence to fill him or her in on discussion items or to provide clarification of the meeting notes.
- When appropriate, subcommittees will be formed to develop proposals for the team's consideration.

Resource

18

Meeting Agenda

Approximate Time

30 minutes for creating the first draft, ongoing use at each meeting.

Attendees/Participants

Meeting chairs, facilitators, and participants.

Purpose

Develop and implement a meeting agenda format that is functional and created by meeting participants.

Directions

1. Explain the value of using a standardized agenda format. A standardized format will help with future reviews of agenda items and notes. It can also be helpful for a supervisor or newcomer to review historical meeting items.
2. Ask each participant to bring copies of an agenda that he or she has used in the past or is currently using and whose format he or she likes.
3. At the next meeting, have attendees distribute and briefly discuss their agendas.
4. Ask members to highlight items on the agendas that they find appealing and applicable.
5. Based on participants' responses, record aspects of the agendas to use for your own agenda format and items to avoid.
6. Develop a first draft of a new agenda.
7. Identify a date to review and revise the new agenda format.

Follow-Up

Mark the review date on your calendar and be sure to include it on the meeting agenda at that time. We suggest scheduling the review six months down the line or before the school year ends, whichever is sooner. Ask meeting participants to conduct the same activity at their grade-level, department, or curriculum team meetings. In time, the entire staff may be ready to adopt a single agenda format. This will considerably reduce the amount of time you need to spend reading agendas and providing feedback to your staff.

The sample format we provide here incorporates several ideas from different staff members involved in creating a new agenda format. All stakeholders followed it and felt ownership of it because they were involved in its development.

Materials

- Meeting agenda.
- Multiple agenda formats to review and critique.

Meeting Agenda

Type of Meeting:

Location:

Date:

Start Time–End Time:

Present:

☐ Name ☐ Name ☐ Name

☐ Name ☐ Name ☐ _____

☐ Name ☐ Name ☐ _____

Topic	Outcome	Person(s) Responsible	Time
Introductions	Learn names of attendees.	All	
Purpose	Identify purpose of the meeting: *Why are we meeting today?*	Facilitator/ Chair	
Agenda	Review agenda and make revisions if necessary.	All	
Adjourn			

Action Items				
Item	Responsibility	Milestone	Status	Done
Date on which action was identified				
What needs to be done	Who will lead it	Due date	Progress made	Yes/No

Notes: _____

_____

_____

_____

Future Meeting Dates—and Note Takers:

September: [Name]   February: [Name]

October: [Name]   March: [Name]

November: [Name]   April: [Name]

December: [Name]   May: [Name]

January: [Name]   June: [Name]

Resource 19

Extracurricular Survey

Approximate Time

Setup and plan of action, one leadership team meeting; filling out the survey, 5 to 10 minutes.

Attendees/Participants

Leadership team and students.

Purpose

Develop and implement a survey to examine students' opinions about extracurricular programs.

Directions

1. Assemble the leadership team to discuss the extracurricular programs your school offers.
2. Discuss the purpose of administering a survey on these programs.
3. Distribute the sample extracurricular survey (see p. 272), and ask the leadership team to suggest items to add or omit.
4. Finalize the survey and select times for implementation.
5. Select a date to review and examine the quality and effectiveness of the survey instrument.
6. Discuss ways to administer the survey to students and collect results. It could be administered to all new students, to students with discipline problems, by the guidance office, as part of the registration process, as part of the withdrawal process, or to graduated students, for example.
7. Review the data with the team or with a committee assembled for that purpose. If you form a special committee, we recommend including sponsors of activities.
8. Consider meeting with the sponsors of the extracurricular programs to share the survey results. The data from the last five statements on the survey should be put into a graph for easy interpretation. Ask the sponsors for suggestions to improve the results. The last five statements can be used to develop numerical tallies and create SMART goals if desired.

Follow-Up

Use the demographic data to determine whether your clubs are reaching students of all grade levels and cultural backgrounds as well as students of both sexes. This area of the survey will also provide quality data to develop data-based goals. You may also want to share the results with a team of student representatives (making sure not to include survey respondents' names). Ask the student team for suggestions to improve participation.

Materials

- Sample extracurricular survey.

Sample Extracurricular Survey

The purpose of this survey is to obtain valuable information about your interests and your opinions on the extracurricular programs at this school. Please take a moment and complete the fields below:

			M F	W B H A O
Last Name	First Name	Grd	Sex	Race (optional)
What extracurricular activities were you involved in last year?	1. 2. 3.			
Are you currently involved in any extracurricular activities? If so, please list the programs.	1. 2. 3.			
If you are not currently involved in extracurricular programs, please explain why and circle any reasons that apply.	Lack of transportation Cost No clubs I like Not interested Other reasons: 1. 2. 3.			

What suggestions do you have for your school to increase student interest in extra-curricular programs?	
What other programs would you like to see offered?	1. 2. 3.

Please respond to the following statements by placing a check mark in the appropriate column on the right.	Strongly Agree	Agree	No Opinion	Disagree	Strongly Disagree
I know what extracurricular programs are available in my school.					
I know whom to contact if I am interested in a particular program.					
The programs are well publicized.					
My friends talk about the programs and clubs they are in.					
I have tried to get involved, but it was too difficult.					

Resource

Resource 20
Open-Ended Questions for Data Discussions

Approximate Time

90 minutes for initial discussion; future discussions ongoing.

Attendees/Participants

Leadership team initially, then all teams and departments.

Purpose

Develop an understanding of meaningful data and a schoolwide culture of data-driven decisions.

Directions

1. Assemble the leadership team or decision-making body at your school.
2. Share the desired outcome of all staff using data to make daily decisions and to help drive the school forward as an entity.
3. Distribute the open-ended questions for data discussions (see p. 275).
4. Ask meeting attendees to independently write responses to the questions in part I.
5. Allow time for attendees to discuss their responses in pairs or triads. The purpose of this segment of the exercise is to help staff members become comfortable talking about data that they already use and are familiar with.
6. Engage attendees in a group discussion about their findings on questions 1–6.
7. Provide attendees with data reports and graphs, if available. Try to use data that they are familiar with as well as samples that they may not know exist. You might consider using the examples in Chapter 7 to generate discussion.
8. Move to part II and ask attendees to think not just about data they currently use or the data that were just shared, but other data as well. Ask them to independently write their responses to question 7, then chart those responses.
9. Ask attendees whether they can combine any responses under such general issues as student attendance, absences, tardies, or discipline issues. Make adjustments as necessary and number each item.
10. Distribute sticky notes to the attendees and ask each one to write down the numbers of his or her top three to five choices of data to address as a school, one per sticky note. Then ask attendees to place their sticky notes by the corresponding items. This will provide a quick visual of a prioritized

list of data to be addressed. Writing the number on the sticky note first helps people stay with the decisions they made independently and helps provide a true perspective of the group's desires. To maintain anonymity, you could also collect the responses first and then post them.

11. Review the results with the attendees and decide on which data need to be addressed first. This should be apparent by the number of sticky notes by each item.

12. Engage attendees in answering questions 8–11, which relate to the identified data to be addressed. If the responses are not positive on these questions, consider moving to the next item on the prioritized list.

13. Develop a plan of action with timelines for implementation and progress, and identify responsibilities in the action plan.

Follow-Up

Mark the calendar to bring the action plan up as an agenda item around the dated timelines. As an extension of this activity, ask meeting attendees to take the same exercise back to their teams or departments and to bring the results of their internal meetings to the next leadership meeting for discussion.

Materials

- Open-ended questions for data discussions.
- Chart paper, whiteboard, overhead projector, or other method of group presentation.
- Sample or real data reports and graphs, preferably from your school.
- Writing utensil for each participant.

Open-Ended Questions for Data Discussions

Part I

1. Which data are driving decisions for the school?

_____

_____

_____

2. Which data are driving decisions for the classroom?

_____

_____

_____

3. Which data do the staff currently refer to and use?

_____

_____

_____

4. Are those data converted into easy-to-understand graphs?

_____

_____

_____

5. Which other data do staff have access to?

_____

_____

_____

6. Which data would staff like to have access to?

_____

_____

_____

Part II

7. Which data would be most important for us to address first?

_____

_____

_____

8. Can we, the stakeholders, change the identified data? In other words, do we agree that we can affect and control these data?

_____

_____

_____

9. Are we confident that we can change these data?

_____

_____

_____

10. Are the data currently disaggregated to be meaningful and understandable enough to develop an action plan for improvement?

_____

_____

_____

11. Which data will be used to measure growth during the implementation of an action plan?

_____

_____

_____

References

Abrutyn, L. (2006). The most important data. *Educational Leadership*, 54–57.

Alliance for Excellent Education. (2005, August). Teacher attrition: A costly loss to the nation and to the states. *Issue Brief*, 1–7.

Anderson, L. W., & Krathwohl, D. (Eds.). (2001). *A taxonomy for learning, teaching, and assessing: A revision of Bloom's Taxonomy of Educational Objectives*. New York: Allyn and Bacon.

Armstrong, T. (2000). *Multiple intelligences in the classroom*. Alexandria, VA: Association for Supervision and Curriculum Development.

Bamburg, J. D. (1994). *Raising expectations to improve student learning*. Urban Monograph Series. Oak Brook, IL: North Central Regional Educational Laboratory.

Barth, R. S. (2002, May). The culture builder. *Educational Leadership, 59*(8), 6–11.

Black, P., & Wiliam, D. (1998, October). Inside the black box: Raising standards through classroom assessment. *Phi Delta Kappan, 80*(2).

Bossidy, L., & Charan, R. (2002). *Execution: The discipline of getting things done*. New York: Crown Business.

Bui, K. (2007, Spring). Educational expectations and academic achievement among middle and high school students. *Education, 127*(3), 328–331.

Campbell, P., & Storo, J. N. (1994). *Girls are. . . Boys are. . . : Myths, stereotypes and gender differences.* Newton, MA: Education Development Center, Inc. Available: www.campbell-kibler.com/stereo.pdf

Collins, J. (2001). *Good to great.* New York: HarperBusiness.

Covey, S. (1997). *The 7 habits of highly effective families.* New York: Golden Books.

Elmore, R. F., & City, E. A. (2007, May/June). The road to school improvement: It's hard, it's bumpy, and it takes as long as it takes. *Harvard Education Letter, 23*(3), 1–3.

Gabriel, J. G. (2005). *How to thrive as a teacher leader.* Alexandria, VA: Association for Supervision and Curriculum Development.

Gardner, J. W. (1990). *On leadership.* New York: The Free Press.

Hetzner, A. (2007, November 8). Data building better teachers. *Milwaukee Journal Sentinel.*

Hoerr, T. R. (2005). *The art of school leadership.* Alexandria, VA: Association for Supervision and Curriculum Development.

Jessness, J. (2002, July). Stand and Deliver *revisited.* Available: www.reason.com/news/show/28479.htm

Katzenbach, J. R., & Smith, D. K. (1993, March/April). The discipline of teams. *Harvard Business Review, 71*(2), 111–120.

Keating, J. (2006). School leadership teams the engine of change. 2006 ASCD Annual Conference Blog. Available: http://ascd.typepad.com/annualconference/2006/04/school_leadersh.html

Keller, B. (2008, March 18). Studies link teacher absences to lower student scores. *Education Week.*

Kline, J. A. (n.d.). Communication and leadership. Article prepared for AU-24, Concepts for Airforce Leadership. Available: www.au.af.mil/au/awc/awcgate/au-24/au24-289.htm

Kouzes, J. M., & Posner, B. Z. (2002). *The leadership challenge* (3rd ed.). San Francisco: Jossey-Bass.

Kuykendall, C. (2004). *From rage to hope: Strategies for reclaiming black and Hispanic students.* Bloomington, IN: Solution Tree.

Marquardt, M. J. (1999). *Action learning in action: Transforming problems and people for world-class organizational learning.* Palo Alto, CA: Davies-Black Publishing.

Marshall, K. (2003, May). Recovery from HSPS (Hyperactive Superficial Principal Syndrome): A progress report. *Phi Delta Kappan,* 701–709.

Marzano, R. J. (2003). *What works in schools: Translating research into action.* Alexandria, VA: Association for Supervision and Curriculum Development.

Marzano, R. J. (2006). *Classroom assessment and grading that work*. Alexandria, VA: Association for Supervision and Curriculum Development.

Marzano, R., Waters, T., & McNulty, B. A. (2005). *School leadership that works: From research to results*. Alexandria, VA: Association for Supervision and Curriculum Development.

Reeves, D. (2000). *Accountability in action: A blueprint for learning organizations*. Advanced Learning Press.

Reeves, D. B. (2006). *The learning leader*. Alexandria, VA: Association for Supervision and Curriculum Development.

Richardson, J. (2002, August/September). Thinking outside of the clock. *Tools for Schools*. National Staff Development Council.

Robbins, P., & Alvy, H. (2004). *The new principal's fieldbook: Strategies for success*. Alexandria, VA: Association for Supervision and Curriculum Development.

Schmoker, M. (2006). *Results now: How we can achieve unprecedented improvements in teaching and learning*. Alexandria, VA: Association for Supervision and Curriculum Development.

Spillane, J. (2006). *Distributed leadership*. San Francisco: Jossey-Bass.

Starratt, R. J. (1995). *Leaders with vision: The quest for school renewal*. Newbury, CA: Corwin Press.

Task Force on Developing Research in Educational Leadership. (2003). *What we know about successful school leadership*. Washington, DC: American Educational Research Association.

Tuckman, B. W. (1965). Developmental sequence in small groups. *Psychology Bulletin, 63*, 384–399. Bethesda, MD: Naval Medical Research Institute.

Vaughn, S. (2002, July 1). *A new era: Revitalizing special education for children and their families*. Washington, DC: President's Commission on Excellence in Special Education.

Waiksnis, M. (2008, January 25). Looks great, but what next? Available: Nasspblogs.org/middleview

The following are the Web sites from which we pulled the different schools' vision and mission statements:

- www.battlefieldhighschool.org/Battlefield%20Info/aboutus.htm
- http://web.montgomeryschoolsmd.org/schools/rmhs/ aboutus/
- www.mcps.k12.md.us/schools/bakerms/SIP/School%20 Improvement%20Plan%202007-2008%2011_11_07.pdf

- www.potomacpanthers.org
- http://brentsvillehs.groupfusion.net/modules/cms/pages.phtml?
  pageid=1455&sessionid=f55f07fdbd55c5a807e32d44cd1f98c7

All vision and mission statements from corporations were pulled from
www.careerbuilder.com.

Index

Note: Information presented in figures is denoted by *f*.

About the Authors

John G. Gabriel is the author of the ASCD best-seller *How to Thrive as a Teacher Leader* (2005) and the article "What It Takes to Make a Teacher Leader" (EQ; 2005). He is currently an assistant principal at Park View High School in Loudoun County, Virginia. He worked in three other public school systems as an English teacher and then as a department chair before entering adminis-tration. He received his bachelor's degree from Mary Washington College, graduating with honors in English and Education. Gabriel also holds a master's degree in Educational Leadership from George Mason University. A nationally known speaker and pre-senter, Gabriel has presented workshops and staff development sessions at ASCD conferences and symposiums and for various school districts. He can be reached at gabrielresearch@msn.com.

Paul C. Farmer started in public education in 1982. During his career, he has worked in public schools in Montgomery County, Maryland, and Fairfax County, Virginia. He is a seasoned school administrator who has successfully implemented affordable school reform strategies. He has held the positions of teacher, support team leader, department chair, teacher specialist, assistant principal, principal, and project director of instructional technology integration in the superintendent's office of Fairfax County Public Schools. He earned his bachelor's degree in Business Management at National Louis University and his master's degree in Educational Leadership from George Mason University. He is the Chief Executive Officer for Leaders in Education Achieving Results Nationwide, LLC (L.E.A.R.N., LLC). He is a seasoned presenter and staff developer, providing educational consulting services to school-based teachers and administrators as well as central office staff in school systems throughout the United States and Canada. Farmer can be reached at pcfarmer @learn4schools.com.

Related ASCD Resources: School Improvement and Leadership

At the time of publication, the following ASCD resources were available (ASCD stock numbers appear in parentheses). For up-to-date information about ASCD resources, go to www.ascd.org.

Multimedia

Creating the Capacity for Change: An ASCD Action Tool by Jody Mason Westbrook and Valarie Spisder-Albert (#702118)

Guide for Instructional Leaders, Guide 1: An ASCD Action Tool (#506138)

Guide for Instructional Leaders, Guide 2: An ASCD Action Tool by Grant Wiggins, John L. Brown, and Ken O'Connor (#703105)

Guide for Instructional Leaders, Guide 3: An ASCD Action Tool by Robby Champion, Anne Meek, and Karen M. Dyer (#703111)

Guiding School Improvement with Action Research Books-in-Action Package (10 Books and 1 video) (#700261)

Making School Improvement Happen with What Works in Schools: An ASCD Action Tool Set (Three Tools) by John L. Brown (#705055)

Schooling by Design: An ASCD Action Tool (#707039)

Networks

Visit the ASCD Web site (www.ascd.org) and click on About ASCD. Go to the section on Networks for information about professional educators who have formed groups around topics such as "Restructuring Schools." Look in the Network Directory for current facilitators' addresses and phone numbers.

Online Courses

Visit the ASCD Web site (www.ascd.org) for the following professional development opportunities:

Contemporary School Leadership by Vera Blake (#PD04OC38)

Creating and Sustaining Professional Learning Communities by Vera Blake and Diane Jackson (#PD04OC43)

What Works in Schools: An Introduction by John Brown (#PD04OC36)

Print Products

Accountability for Learning: How Teachers and School Leaders Can Take Charge by Douglas B. Reeves (#104004)

Align the Design: A Blueprint for School Improvement by Nancy J. Mooney and Ann T. Mausbach (#108005)

Connecting Leadership with Learning: A Framework for Reflection, Planning, and Action by Michael Copland and Michael Knapp (#105003)

Education Update, September 2003: Teacher Leadership in Urban Schools (#103394)

Educational Leadership, September 2007: Teachers as Leaders (#108020)

Educational Leadership, May 2006: Challenging the Status Quo (#106043)

Educational Leadership, February 2005: How Schools Improve (#105032)

Enhancing Professional Practice: A Framework for Teaching (2nd ed.) by Charlotte Danielson (#106034)

Enhancing Student Achievement: A Framework for School Improvement by Charlotte Danielson (#102109)

How to Thrive as a Teacher Leader by John G. Gabriel (#104150)

Leadership Capacity for Lasting School Improvement by Linda Lambert (#102283)

Leadership for Learning: How to Help Teachers Succeed by Carl D. Glickman (#101031)

The Learning Leader: How to Focus School Improvement for Better Results by Douglas B. Reeves (#105151)

The Results Fieldbook: Practical Strategies from Dramatically Improved Schools by Mike Schmoker (#101001)

Results Now: How We Can Achieve Unprecedented Improvements in Teaching and Learning by Mike Schmoker (#106045)

School Money Matters: A Handbook for Principals by Davida W. Mutter and Pam J. Parker (#103057)

Schooling by Design: Mission, Action, and Achievement by Grant Wiggins and Jay McTighe (#107018)

Teacher Leadership That Strengthens Professional Practice by Charlotte Danielson (#105048)

Transforming Schools: Creating a Culture of Continuous Improvement by Allison Zmuda, Robert Kuklis, and Everett Kline (#103112)

Video and DVD

What Works in Schools (DVD and Facilitator's Guide) (#603047)

Leadership Strategies for Principals (DVD and *The New Principal's Fieldbook: Strategies for Success* by Pam Robbins and Harvey Alvy) (#608033)

The Results Video Series (DVD and Online Facilitator's Guide) (#601261)

A Visit to a Data-Driven School District (DVD and Viewer's Guide) (#606059)

The Whole Child Initiative helps schools and communities create learning environments that allow students to be healthy, safe, engaged, supported, and challenged. To learn more about other books and resources that relate to the whole child, visit www.wholechildeducation.org.

For more information: send e-mail to member@ascd.org; call 1-800-933-2723 or 703-578-9600, press 2; send a fax to 703-575-5400; or write to Information Services, ASCD, 1703 N. Beauregard St., Alexandria, VA 22311-1714 USA.